Social Dynamics in Contemporary North-East India

ABOUT THE AUTHORS

Dr. Shukhdeba Sharma Hanjabam was born on 28th February 1983 in India's North Eastern State of Manipur. He received his Ph.D. from the School of Social Work, Tata Institute of Social Sciences Mumbai. Presently, he is associated as Assistant Professor, Department of Social Work, Indira Gandhi National Tribal University, Regional Campus, Manipur. He has the first-hand experiences and exposure to Self-Determination Movements; Human Rights and Conflict situations in North-east India particularly Manipur. His main interest is Social Work and Political Conflict and Human Security.

He can be contacted at **hanjabam@gmail.com**.

Prof. J.J. Roy Burman was born in Kolkata, India in 1955. After graduating in Anthropology from Calcutta University, he received his Masters in Sociology and Social Anthropology from North Bengal University, Darjeeling, and his Ph.D. at Tata Institute of Social Sciences, Mumbai. Roy Burman worked on an Indo-NORAD watershed project in the Himalayas, Uttaranchal. As a Research Fellow of the Centre for Research in Rural and Industrial Development, Chandigarh, he did a study on Counter-insurgency problems in Mizoram in 1981. Subsequently, he served with Help Age India as a Project Adviser being in-charge of East and North-East India. Since July 1988, he is working with Tata Institute of Social Sciences, Mumbai. His work entails teaching and doing research besides guiding a number of Masters, M. Phil. and Ph.D. Scholars. Presently, he is at the School of Social Sciences.

His research work has mainly been field based stressing on issues of North-east India, tribal problems in different parts of the country. He has published around 60 papers and four books. They mostly cover experiences of ethnicity and Environmental management. He has attended a number of national and international seminars and conferences.

He can be contacted at **jnanjyoti55@yahoo.co.in, burman@tiss.edu.**

Social Dynamics in Contemporary North-East India

A Study of Regional Exclusion, Self-Determination Movements and Ethnic Violence

Shukhdeba Sharma Hanjabam
J.J. Roy Burman

CONCEPT PUBLISHING COMPANY PVT. LTD.
NEW DELHI-110059

ISBN-13: 978-81-8069-939-9

First Published 2013

Published and Printed by

Concept Since 1974

Concept Publishing Company Pvt. Ltd.
A/15-16, Commercial Block, Mohan Garden
New Delhi-110059 (India)
T: 25351460, 25351794, *F*: 091-11-25357109
E: publishing@conceptpub.com, W: www.conceptpub.com
Editorial Office: H-13, Bali Nagar, New Delhi-110 015, India.

Cataloging in Publication Data--*Courtesy:* D.K. Agencies (P) Ltd. <docinfo@dkagencies.com>

Hanjabam, Shukhdeba Sharma, 1983-
Social dynamics in contemporary North-East India : a study of regional exclusion, self-determination movements and ethnic violence / Shukhdeba Sharma Hanjabam, J.J. Roy Burman.
p. cm.
Includes bibliographical references and index.
ISBN 9788180699399

1. Marginality, Social—India, Northeastern. 2. Self-determination, National—India, Northeastern. 3. Ethnic conflict—India, Northeastern. 4. India, Northeastern Politics and government. I. Roy Burman, J. J., 1955-, joint author. II. Title.

DDC 305.5609541 23

Preface

Social Exclusion refers to the process and outcome of keeping social groups outside power centres and resources. Social exclusion is a discriminatory practice which leads to segregation of people from social, political, economic, cultural, educational and religious domains of life. It also leads to a notion superiority and inferiority among the members of the same society or culture. All these ultimately cause a position of oppression and exploitation.

North-East India is one such region in India which feels excluded from rest of the country. It is not just a matter of feeling but almost all development indicators point towards a position of utter backwardness. It is revealed that the road length per 100 sq km of North-East is higher than the national average (114.73 km) in the States of Assam (114.09 km), Nagaland (126.79 km) and Tripura (155.41 km). But the road length per lakh population for Assam is 9.5, the national average is 135.6. There is hardly any presence of railways in other States of North-East. There has virtually been no expansion of the route km per 100 sq km between 2001 and 2005 in all the States of North-East except for Tripura (4.3 km to 6.1 km). In fact, there has been a slight fall in the Assam figure (32.1 to 32). The national average went up from 700.4 to 709.9 during the same period.

The Net State Domestic Product (NSDP) data comparison between the national figures and the North-East displays a dismal picture for the latter except for the primary sector. The Compound Growth Rates of NSDP per capita of different States of North-East reveals that except for Assam, Manipur and Meghalaya, NSDP growth rates are above or close to the national average of 5.1 per cent.

However, the NSDP growth rate for the major State of the region, Assam is very dismal picture of disparity in comparison with the all-India average.

Apart from these, a major factor of discrimination of North-East lies in the Parliamentary form of democracy in which the population logic of constituency formation has directly marginalised the people of the region. Consequently, it is seen that while the eight States of North-East are represented by 25 seats in the Lok Sabha, Uttar Pradesh alone is represented by 80 seats in the same house. Again in case of Arunachal Pradesh, while it is just 1,000 hectares smaller in size than West Bengal, it has only one seat in Lok Sabha, the latter has 42 seats.

There are many factors which can be attributed to the reasons behind the self-determination movements in the entire North-East region. Of them the regional exclusion dimension is perhaps one of the most crucial one. People feel being deprived of and lagging behind as compared to other regions of the country. People consequently feel neglected. But apart from being neglected, there are many other factors which have been given birth to so many movements of self-determination in the region.

Hanjabam "Roots of Self-Determination Movements in India's North-East", discusses this at length. The self-determination movements were witnessed in the State of Manipur in the late 40s, Nagaland in the 40s, Mizoram and Tripura in the 60s and Assam in the late 70s. Meghalaya and Arunachal are more of resting place for the bigger resistance groups. The demand by the resistance groups can be broadly divided between independence or secession and Autonomy or anything beyond Independence. Binalakshmi Nepram observed that the region has become the "South Asia Fractured Frontier". The intention of this book is to cover only the root causes of the armed self-determination movement. But it also gives the present situation of the movements. The book begins with Manipur and is followed by the States of Nagaland, Mizoram, Assam and Tripura. Arunachal and Meghalaya are not considered in this book.

To him, historical reasons are very important and also the process of State formation itself is at the roots of political disturbance of Manipur. He argues that Manipur was never a part of India and it was only notionally colonised by the British. Hence, after departure of British, the Manipuris had every right to form an independent country and which incidentally formed. A separate Parliament with a separate

Constitution too was formed. But India denied to accept these and a force merger was thrust. In the process, the independence of Manipur which tries to balance between the different tribes and the Meitei community got disturbed. The force hegemony led to Meitei domination in the government.

Hanjabam further goes on to show that the Government of India has used draconian legal means to help the security force to coerce the people to submission. Many innocent lives have been lost in the process and property has been destroyed. The Armed Forces Special Powers Act 1958 of the State which has permitted even any ordinary security forces to shoot any person on suspicion even to the extent of death. Many people have now stood up against this Act by means of peaceful protests, strikes and fast. Irom Sharmila is worth mentioned as she has been protesting with an indefinite hunger strike since 2000.

While discussing about the issue of self-determination, Hanjabam also locates large scale immigration of outsiders from different parts of the country as well as Bangladesh and Nepal, to be serious factors of arousing negative feelings among the indigenous peoples. Other than these, Hanjabam also holds fight for autonomy as reason for self-determination movements according to him. The Bodos, Karbis, Kukis, Hmar and Dimasa, etc., are involved in the self-determination movement according to him.

J.J. Roy Burman in his article "Ethnic Violence in North-East India", has indicated that violence in the region occurs not only between the State and the indigenous peoples, but also believe different ethnic entities. These skirmishes are mainly due to fight over natural resources and political control. Quite often the colonial powers and the Indian State has formulated trouble between the ethnic entities like the Kukis and the Nagas or Bodos or the Assamese. Sometimes, international forces across border too have encouraged such trouble. They also armed the different groups with small arms and sophisticated weapons. Many of the militant groups took shelter in the adjoining countries of the North-East and trained themselves. But the State itself is alleged to have armed different faction for counter-insurgency purpose. The NSCN-Khaplang in Nagaland, the SULFA and BdSF in Assam are believed to have some heavily funded and trained by the Indian Army and other security apparatus.

The violence perpetrated by the State was of various kinds. Combing operations were of drastic nature. Men, women, children and even the old were brought out of their homes and made to stand in the open field for hours together. Quite often the houses were torched so as to destroy the foodstock. Religious spaces were defied. many a time women were molested and raped with impunity. Nagaland and Mizoram witnessed aerial bombing and regrouping of villages into concentration camps. The group in centres have now turned out to be unplanned urban centres with no economic base.

It is, however, seen that violence in the region is rather on the wane. The State has engaged itself with different militant groups and come into certain peace treaties. Though such treaties are themselves wrought with controversies, like the Meiteis are strongly opposed to the treaty between the NSCN (IM) and Government of India over the issue of non-territorial order or the Paresh Baruah faction of ULFA is opposed to current treaty with others led by Arabinda Rajkhiwa over the clause of sovereignty. Roy Burman argued that the violence perpetuated in North-East India is not 'violence *per se*' but is a reaction to the State intrusion and violence entertained by it.

The three articles in the volume are largely centering on these perspectives.

Acknowledgements

We are very grateful to Prof. Amar Yumnam, Director, Centre for Manipur Studies, Manipur University, for allowing us to reproduce the working paper: Regional Exclusion with particular reference to North-East India (Working Paper New Series No.1, September 2010, Centre for Manipur Studies, Manipur University).

And

Dr. M.C. Arun, Department of Anthropology, Manipur University for his thoughtful discussions that help us in refining the title of the book.

Contents

List of Tables

List of Figures and Charts

1

Regional Exclusion with Particular Reference to North-East India

J.J. Roy Burman and *Shukhdeba S. Hanjabam*

Introduction

The issue of Social Exclusion in India is usually treated in terms of caste, tribe, and religion. Consequently, the phenomenon of Regional Exclusion finds little attention. However, it is felt that Regional Exclusion holds a crucial niche in the study of the conflicts confronted by the nation-state. In fact, regional feelings diffuse the sharpness of the ethnic and class conflicts to a great extent. In this chapter at first a modest attempt has been made to stress that the formation of nation-states itself leads to Regional Exclusion, with the dominant ethnic entity enjoying greater powers and say in the political, economical and cultural affairs. It is explicit that this disparity is structural and not procedural. Illustrations from few Balkan nations and West Africa have been presented to initiate the dialogue. Next, this has been further stretched to elucidate the all-round Social Exclusion witnessed by the North Eastern part of India regionally. A number of development indicators have been depicted along with qualitative information and analysis for validification.

The discourse on social exclusion, discrimination and identity formation has gained immense importance in India at present. According to Prakash Louis (n.d.) Social Exclusion refers to the process and outcome of keeping social groups outside power centres and resources. Social exclusion is a discriminatory practice. In the course of human development, exclusion has taken the form of segregating a group of people from the social, political, economic, cultural, educational and religious domains of social life. But social exclusion does not limit itself to segregation and deprivation. Social exclusion and isolation provide a base for a sense of superiority and inferiority among members of the same society or culture. It also culminates into a system of domination and subjugation. All these processes ultimately lead to oppression and exploitation.

The concept of social exclusion has been treated very broadly by different scholars and it is very difficult to arrive at an exact definition of the concept. According to Arjan de Haan (Louis: *ibid.*), the concept has two main defining characteristics. First, it is a multidimensional concept. People may be excluded from livelihoods, employment, earnings, property, housing, minimum consumption, education, the welfare state, citizenship, personal contacts or respect, etc. But the concept focuses on the multidimensionality of deprivation, on the fact that people are often deprived of different things at the same time. It refers to exclusion (deprivation) in the economic, social and political sphere. Second, social exclusion implies a focus on the relations and processes that cause deprivation. People can be excluded by many different sorts of groups, often at the same time: landlords exclude people from access to land or housing; elite political groups exclude others from legal rights; priests in India may exclude Scheduled Castes from access to temples; minorities may be excluded from expressing their identity; labour markets, as also some trade unions exclude people (non-members) from getting jobs.

The essence of social exclusion can be first traced back to the biblical sense when Adam and Eve were excluded from Paradise having failed to comply to the rules of Eden and God. Until then both Adam and Eve were part of Eden and both were equal in status and position. Subsequently, tribes and groups of individuals collectively acted together for the good and survival of the community but with little affiliation with fellow communities. These groups later developed into nations and subsequently into empires. Much later Plato in his political work "*I nomoi*" distinguishes the artisans and farmers from citizens on the ground that being a citizen is a full-time job, superior to all others. He then ranks people in three quality groups. In the first group and of the highest quality he placed the philosophers, followed by the citizens and then came the artisans and farmers and finally completely excludes women and slaves, stressing that they should have neither any political nor any social rights. In the Middle Ages and between the XII to the XIX centuries, the socially excluded were those people considered unacceptable by the church. This group included killers, thieves, the poverty-stricken (known as paupers), certain occupations such as butchers, decorators, mercenaries, women, the physically and mentally handicapped, the elderly, the prostitutes, the beggars, etc. Later, when power shifted to the monarchies other figures were added and shifts in the criteria for assigning social exclusion took place. For example, peasants and farm hands were added in order to fighting wars and fuel in local military campaigns and also rival political and monarchy figures were included (Ward and Farmaki: 2006)

The term social exclusion as such, had arisen in France in the 60s and 70s. It first appeared in Pierre Masse's report *Les dividends du progres*. Almost at the same time J. Klanfer published on the same concept in *L'exclusion sociale*. However, Rene Lenoir, is considered to be the inventor of the modern interpretation of social exclusion as in his 1974 publication titled *Les Exclus, un Français sur Dix* (The excluded, one Frenchman in ten) he refers to groups of people not covered by the traditional social security system. But Lenoir was not very explicit with the concept of exclusion. During the 1980s and the 1990s, the idea of social exclusion became widely adopted in the European Union, as because certain governments of Europe harboured reservations about the word 'poverty' when applied to their respective countries in the programmes of poverty. In the "Green Book" of the EU, the term is used as a synonym of poverty, unemployment, discrimination and racism, because it is thought that long-term unemployment is what creates the exclusion from the labour market, where racism and discrimination create, or perhaps complete, social exclusion. The notion of 'social exclusion' is considered to be multidimensional and much wider than poverty. It speaks both in terms of economic position as well as social relations (Ward and Farmiki: *ibid.*). Sonowal (2008) argues that exclusion can be studied both in terms of individuals and groups: "Group based disadvantages give rise to 'horizontal' model of inequality where inequalities in question cut across economically defined strata and differentiate the ability of different groups and categories within society to access valued resources and opportunities".

According to R.R. Singh (2003), the term social exclusion, first used in Europe, finds its parallel in poverty, inequality, deprivation, alienation and marginalization in the developing countries. Social stratification in India is also its example. Social exclusion, in the European context, has been defined in relation to social rights of citizens to retain basic standards of living and to participation in the major social and occupational opportunities of the society. In their contribution to the World Summit on Social Development, Gerry Rodgers *et al.* (1995) have pointed to the trend of transnationalisation of social and economic life and the interrelationship between poverty, productive employment and social integration. They have identified various forms of exclusion, namely, exclusion from goods and services, labour markets, land security (both physical and environmental security), security of livelihood, protection against contingencies (illness/death), security of livelihood, protection against contingencies (illness/death), human rights and macro-economic development strategies. The 1998 Annual Report of the World Bank describes social exclusion as a "process through which individuals and groups are wholly or partially excluded from full economic, political and cultural participation in the society in which they live". It also points to the services and social safety. A multi-pronged strategy for social protection adopted by Bank includes protection against loss of income through old age and unemployment, help to the unemployed in finding jobs, job placements, training and public works, regulation of labour markets to provide gainful employment; social assistance, technical assistance (pension reform), social fund (grant for locally generated social development efforts), and special income support for displaced workers in order to combat poverty which may be marginal, incidental or structural 'feminised or juvenised'.

Thus, taking into consideration of the broad parameters, 'social exclusion' primarily means exclusion from:

- Power structure of the polity;
- Participation in social and ritual life with equal status and dignity;
- Enjoyment on an equity principle the right to access to the endowments of nature and other life support resources;
- Enjoyment on equity principle the traits of social production and conveniences and services available to the citizens;
- Enjoyment of equity principles and social goods and cultural goods available to citizens;

- Participation with same right and dignity as proffered to other segments of the society in the process of decision-making in matters of common interest for the society;
- Enjoyment of the right legally due to people.

Regional Exclusion

Ward and Farmiki (2006) state that social exclusion may occur in terms of geographical spaces as well, "This implies the socially excluded are fenced within specific boundaries, living within geographical margins and consequently isolated from the centre or core, i.e., where the rest of the society lives and where they should be living in order to be considered included". In Nigeria it has been noticed that regionalism plays a much greater role than ethnicity in the burgeoning conflicts (Edozie: 2007). The phenomenon of regional exclusion in the context of studies on social exclusion has rather been neglected. In the context of countries like India social exclusion has more been studied by categorizing groups of people based on the principles of caste and ethnicity—tribes and religious minorities. This has led to a fallacious understanding of the social realities witnessed by the nation-state. It is not realized by many that regionalism seriously impedes upon formation of a unified front of the *Dalits* to confront the menace of caste. To a Naga from the North-East it is immaterial whether an Indian in front of him belongs to a Brahmin or *Dalit* caste. To him while the other is an Indian, he himself is a Naga (May not be an Indian) first and foremost.

It is argued here that the moment a nation-state is evolved; it leads to regional exclusion even if not intended. This often leads to movements of right to self-determination. This has been most pronounced in the former Eastern Bloc countries of the Balkans. The case of Yugoslavia is an ideal illustration. The problem there was not so much the suppression of nationalities (With the exception of the Albanians of Kossovo) as the segmental structure of the state and of the Yugoslav Peoples Party (The local communists), which together constituted a ready-made institutional order available first to opportunistic local elites bent on resisting the democratizing of the system and second to those who would oppose them in the name of reform. The self-determination movements and Balkanization drives have led to mass population displacements, torture, murder and political rape forestalling any future peace (Foreman: 1998). In

Yugoslavia in spite avowal to racial equity saw the Serbian predominance. The Croats complained of predominance of Serbian words in the Serb-Croat language, about the representation in politics and the media and about control of institutions like banks. In 1971, the Croat literary society 'Matica Hrvatska' published statistics to support these arguments, showing that Croats were underrepresented in the League of Yugoslavian Communists (Eller: 1999). In Latin America where nation-states have been formed most arbitrarily through the history of colonial conquests, the indigenous peoples are waking up to the call of self-determination. In Peru for instance, the Inca tribes are getting aligned to ethnic organizations to counter the assimilationist campaigns of the post-colonial nation-state (Greene: 2008).

The Kurds, inhabitants of Kurdistan—an area which falls within the contiguous terrain of Iraq, Iran and Turkey have witnessed turbulence for long time in history. Once a part of the Ottoman Empire, the Kurd land has been divided within the ambits of the three nation-states. In each of the state, the Kurds lead a life of exclusion. They are subjected to brutality and discrimination from all the respective states. During the 1991 Gulf war, as many as half-million Kurds fled to Turkey and 1.5 million to Iran. The Kurd areas were Arabized as Arab settlers were transferred into Kurdish majority areas and Kurdish villagers were transferred out to "cluster villages", ostensibly to provide better housing and services to them but also to disperse them and to put them within easy surveillance. In several attacks the Iraqi army had slaughtered hundreds of Kurds. On March 16, 1988, five thousand Kurds died due to bombing of poison gas on Halabja village. The Kurds of Mahabad in Iran too had earlier revolted against the nation-state with the help of the Soviets. The Kurds in both Iran and Iraq fought against their native states with the assistance of the enemy nations. In Turkey, the Kurds fared no better and their lands were militarized and lands expropriated to settle Turks. The Kurdish language was banned and Kurdish organizations banned (Eller: *op. cit.*).

The problems that we get to see in Yugoslavia, Kurd inhabited areas or the Latin American countries are in reality an outcome of the exploitative mechanisms of the centre over the periphery. E. Shils (1975) argues that the core of society is the central value system which has a sacred character and is the ultimate source of authority, legitimating the distribution of wealth, rewards and roles in the social system. While various social elites are fundamentally involved in the centre, other social groups are located at the periphery. As the means of communication are improved with industrialization, the centre becomes more extensive within society and previously peripheral groups become increasingly involved in the central value system and subjected to its authority. The emergence of the modern state was thus a condition for the extension of the centre, the creation of national identity and citizenship right. However, the increasing complexity of modern society and the differentiation of roles means that consensus over central values is always partial and problematic (The Penguin Dictionary of Sociology: 1984, New York).

The iniquitous relationship between the centre and the periphery has been articulated by A.G. Frank (The exponent of the Dependency theory) long back. He draws a "metropolis-satellite" analogy to denote the powerful centre out of which innovations emerge and a dependent hinterland held in its sway. He spoke of the chain of exploitation—or the flow and appropriation of capital through successive metropolis-satellite relationships, each of which participates in the perpetuation of relative inequalities even while experiencing some enrichment. Galtung characterized this same relationship in terms of "core and periphery", each with something to offer to the other, thereby fostering a symbiotic but lopsided relationship. The effect is an intersocietal hierarchy in which the dominant core grows and becomes more complex, while the satellite is subordinated through the transfer of economic surpluses to the core in spite whatever absolute economic changes may be realized (Ahmed and Biswas: 2004).

The centre-periphery concept and the dependency theories both lead to the concept of internal colonization. While the former mainly targets the global hegemonic forces, the internal colonization concept by and large indicts the exploitative processes of the newly independent states of the South. "The earliest sense referred to physical conquest within, not across, political boundaries. Lenin used the concept way back in 1896 to describe the Tsarist autocracy's creation by force of the Russian Empire as an internal market for capital centred in St. Petersburg and Moscow. In a similar sense, the Nordic Institute of Asian Studies used 'internal colonisation' in 1996 to refer to the physical conquest of the non-Han peoples in China by the Government of the People's Republic. It thus designates a process by which large parts of many Southern states (and of the countryside in some Northern ones) are still in effect being colonized by their own ruling elite; whether political or economic reasons do not matter, since the two are in fact inseparable.... In the South, as the indigenous elites replaced the external domination, traditional subsistence agriculture was replaced by large farms or plantations managed for the export and/or commercial sale of a single product or limited range of products. Decolonization often merely replaced foreign owners by local ones enjoying the key advantage of direct access to the centres of political power, and the vogue for socialist style economies in the years following independence gave the ruling elite control over the assets that they did not themselves own".

India has been no exception to the process of internal colonization and this manifests best through the comparison of development indicators between regions of the country and the differences between various parts within different States. It is not surprising that many of the regionally excluded areas have been clamouring either for autonomy or separate statehood. The cases of the Telengana region in Andhra Pradesh, Vidarbha in Maharashtra, Gorkhaland and Kamtapur in West Bengal or Kutch in Gujarat are some of the best illustrations. The leaders of Kutch irrespective of their political party background stress on the cultural difference and distance from Gandhinagar—the State capital as reasons for their demand for separate statehood. They are also peeved by the fact that while Kutch district pays taxes to the tune of over Rs. 600 crore to the State government, the latter spends only about Rs. 200 crores in the district. Besides, the promise made by the government in 1960 to establish an autonomous development board under Article 371 (2) of the Constitution has not been fulfilled till now (Hiral Dave: 2009).

Though Telengana is one of the most resource rich regions of Andhra Pradesh, it remains to be the most backward part of the State. The percentage of literate population in Telengana continues to be the lowest in Andhra Pradesh—57.7 per cent as compared to 66.2 per cent in south coastal Andhra, 61.1 per cent in Rayalaseema and 79.0 per cent in the capital city. The literacy percentage is lowest for Mahabubnagar district at 29.58. The power, irrigation and employment scenario too is the worst within the entire State. As a result, there have been agitations in Telengana, from time to time, for an independent existence and separate identity. The Naxalite movement has also acquired an extremely virulent form in the region (Jairath and Sajja: 2009).

Regional Exclusion with Particular Reference to North-Eastern India

The feeling of political and social exclusion of the people of North-East India from the rest of India is perhaps most intense only next to the Muslim natives of Jammu and Kashmir. Manipur was never a part of India in the history and it was conquered by the British. The British left the state under the control of the King of Manipur. But the Government of India under the initiative of Sardar Vallabh Bhai Patel forcibly annexed Manipur by coercing the King to sign the merger agreement. Partly due to this history and partly because of the indifferent attitude of the Government of India till today, the Centre has been unable to win the complete confidence of the Manipuris. Recently due to insensitive and casual handling of the situation, the State witnessed unprecedented violence and massive popular protest against the extension of the cease fire agreement between the Government of India and the NSCN-IM (An underground Naga militant outfit), without taking into confidence of the majority people in Manipur. As many as fourteen people died in firing by the security forces during the agitation (Brara: 2009). Kunal Chattopadhyay *et al.* (2005) reiterate about the forced conquest of Manipur by the Government of India. The Kangla fort in Imphal, from where the kings of Manipur used to rule, was brought under military control in 1949 and retained till a couple of years back. As a result of savage exploitation and decades of uneven development, national liberation struggles have raised their heads. They are based on the struggles for self-determination. All shades of mainstream parties in India have flatly rejected the right of the people of Manipur to self-determination.Though not exactly in this manner, the other parts of North-East too were annexed in the colonial and post-independence period. In this article we seek to present the different ways the region is excluded from the rest of the Indian nation-state.

A. Political Marginalization

The Indian state, perhaps as a legacy from its colonizers the British, adopted the model of western concept of nationhood and tried to construct its national history and consequently framed the Nation-State a single narrative (Kiswar: 1999). The Indian experience of building of nation-state is much more complex and distinct in some crucial aspects as India presents a picture of one of the most complex multi-ethnic societies in the world governed by a modern nation-state. As the State began to expand and defend its national interest, it sought to homogenize the society in terms of political culture of a nation. In its efforts to unite the diverse groups within its territory into a single whole, the State tried to impose a national culture. It adopted a national language—Hindi.

The democratic order of the Indian nation-state marginalized the small States throughout the country and particularly the North Eastern States—adhering to the population logic in forming the constituencies—a vestige of the colonial era. It is a veritable fact that the India we know today was born on 15th August, 1947. It is a creation of colonial history. But without realising these, the civilizational dimension of India has been imposed over the entire country. A logical and just political arrangement would not have otherwise permitted formation of a Parliament with unequal representation from different States. In a just federal structure all the States should have had equal representation in the Lok Sabha (Roy Burman: 2001). But it is not seen in the Indian federalism and no wonder Sanjib Baruah called it as *"cosmetic federalism"* (Baruah: 2005).

It is a fact that though North-East has a large territory, its population is scanty and the density of population is considerably lower than the rest of the country. Based on the colonial legacy of constituency formation, the region has very few seats in the Lok Sabha. While the State of Uttar Pradesh alone has 80 seats in the Lok Sabha, the entire North-East comprising of eight States has only 25 seats. A State like Nagaland or Mizoram has only one seat. Consequently, they have hardly any say in the political process of the country. Mukhim (*op. cit.*) too writes, "North-East India does not have the requisite number of representatives in Parliament who can turn the spotlight on the region. Since democracy is about numbers, those who lack in numbers also lack the clout to make things happen". This automatically leads to the neglect of the region. The political parties too fall in line. At one time when the BJP was in a very good position to form a government in Manipur by enlisting the allegiance of the MLAs belonging to Samata Party (Its NDA partner at the Centre), it was compelled not to do so fearing withdrawal of the Samata Party support at the Centre. This led to a political precipitation in the State and President's rule was imposed subsequently. Madhab

(1999: 321) similarly writes, "While the North-East has a land area of about 8 per cent, but people's representation in the Parliament is only 4 per cent. This may not be a tenable argument. But there is an element of truth in it. Take for instance, Mizoram; it has only one MP in the Lok Sabha. The system being what it is, he may get to speak only once in five years. This is totally unacceptable. Entire Mizoram may remain unheard".

This apprehension gets reiterated by the fact that a few years back the MPs Jayanta Rongpi of Assam and Sibu Soren of Jharkhand Mukti Morcha of Bihar (now Jharkhand State) walked out of the Parliament in protest due to the fact that they were allowed to speak only for two minutes during the no confidence motion (since the time is allowed as per the number of seats different parties have in their Parliament). So hypothetically the representation of a regional party from Nagaland or Mizoram can never hope to get equal status from other more populated States of the country (Roy Burman: 1999). What is true for Nagaland or Mizoram is true for all the States in the North East India. It is worth mentioning to quote the passing of the controversial Armed Forces Special Act 1958 (AFSPA) in 1958. In spite, of referring the Bill to a Joint Parliamentary Committee to examine the statute and discussing the same in details, on 18th August, 1958, the AFSPA was adopted after a just two hours long summary debate by the Parliament. Many MPs including from Assam and both the MPs from Manipur had opposed the Bill as it was felt to be an invocation of unproclaimed emergency through the backdoor. However, majority of the ruling Congress got the Bill passed (Sanajaoba: 2006).

Table 1.1: Representation of North Eastern State in the Indian Parliament and State Assembly

State	*Lok Sabha—543 (House of the People)*	*Rajya Sabha (Council of States)*
Arunachal Pradesh	2	1
Assam	14	7
Manipur	2	1
Meghalaya	2	1
Mizoram	1	1
Nagaland	1	1
Tripura	2	1
Sikkim	1	1

Source: Baruah, 2006.

The lack of proper autonomy of the people of North-East can be gauged from the fact that there has been very frequent intervention into the affairs of the States by the Central Government. A great deal of power has been delegated to the Governors of the States. Many of the Governors have been appointed due to their experience of serving the security forces. "As appointees of the Central Government and as facilitating agents in the counter-insurgency regime, such antecedence serve very practical ends, particularly in ensuring that the demands of security override the rules of democracy in the event of a conflict between them" (Baruah: 2005). Rudolph & Rudolph (2008) write, "Governors have also abused their discretion with respect to the imposition of President's rule under Article 356 of the Constitution, which allows governors to advise the President that the 'government of (a) State cannot be carried on in accordance with the provisions of the Constitution. Such advice enables the governing party at the Centre to take over the government of a State. In the words of D.D. Basu (Rudolph and Rudolph: *ibid.*)), a leading Constitutional authority, "use of this drastic coercive power takes the substance away from the normal federal polity described by the Constitution. Instead of being a matter of last resort, Article 356 has been used sixty-five times by March 1982". Not surprisingly, very often the State governments have been pulled down on slightest pretexts and President's rule been imposed on them in the North-East. In Manipur alone, President's rule has been imposed eleven times since 1972. The cumulative period of governance under President's rule in the State is no less than three years altogether.

B. Development and Marginalization

The adoption of the Mahalanobis Model (MM)—that of developing the heavy capital intensive industries right after independence itself led to regional inequalities. Sengupta (2005) writes, "Heavy industrialization meant that investment per worker in the concerned industries would be high. Thus, very few well-paid people would be employed, meaning that increase in income would accrue to very few. This meant a greater degree of inequality than what an investment, based on comparative advantage (In India's case abundant labour) would have implied. Secondly, as this high-wage employment was more regionally concentrated than the results of the latter strategy would have been; regional inequality also rose. As the Central

Government set up industries in those regions possessing raw materials required for heavy industry or those that already possessed an industrial base, other regions were at a disadvantage".

In case of North-East India though there is a base of raw materials, heavy industries never got a priority—mainly on grounds of national security and distance from the national markets. Today, 2,62,000 sq km is linked to the Indian mainland through a slender 21 km Siliguri Corridor popularly known as "Chicken Neck". Instead the development activities of the North-East Region are entrusted to the Ministry of Home Affairs who looks after the security of the country. Creation of North-East Council (NEC) clearly illustrated it. When the North-East Council (NEC) was formed in 1971 in order to "act as an advisory body in respect of socio-economic development and balanced development of the North Eastern Areas" it was placed under the Ministry of Home Affairs. Initially only the State Governors were members of the North-East Council. Similarly, when the Department for Development of the North Eastern Region (DONER) was created in 2001 and subsequently upgraded to a full-fledged Ministry in 2004, it was also placed within the Ministry of Home Affairs.

After the creation of Ministry, International Financial Institutions (IFIs) have been seeking deeper penetration into the region where the awareness of the records of the IFIs is less known and the space to seek democratic oversight and accountability are weak. This is observable with the increasing number of projects including many in the pipeline in different sectors. Trans-Asian Railways, Trans-Asian Highways, Mining, Dams—in spite of the highest seismic zone, are few that can be mentioned here. Despite the formation of this Ministry, the Government of India (Allocation of business) Rules did not give overall 'nodal responsibility' for the region to DONER—this continues with the Ministry of Home Affairs. This politics of economic issues has reached its height recently with the requirement of certificates from the Home Ministry for the provincial government to get funds sanctioned from the Ministry of Finance (Yumnam: 2005).

The process of planned economic development has largely bypassed the North-East—at least in spirit. The first to the Tenth Year Plans of North Eastern States have undoubtedly been made in the State capitals. But the absence of a debate on the plans points to the default of local participants in the meaningful way, thereby rendering it largely a bureaucratic exercise (Editorial, *Eastern Quarterly*: 2005). When India started the process of intense industrialization for the transformation of the country starting from the Second Five Year Plan, the North-East region was almost totally neglected. Sengupta (2005) writes that in the initial stages, the heavy industries needed State support to make them viable. To protect the industry, India had to impose high tariffs on industrial imports. As high tariffs were taken recourse to, agriculture was discriminated against, as the price farmers now paid for industrial goods became higher because of the terms of trade effect. This enhanced the regional inequality of North-East as it was fully dependent on the agricultural sector for sustenance. The capital driven development was concentrated in certain specific locations in central India while the North-East as a region continued to suffer from a perpetuation of the logic of underdevelopment. End of British domination in the sub-continent in the post-Second World War era did not produce any path breaking change as the region continued to reel under similar conditions in the face of the external market, now in the form of mainland India market and its emergent national capitalist class. Manipur falls under the category of *"No industrial districts"* by all-India standard. Virtual absence of industrial infrastructure compelled the region to depend only on the primary sector of production even after five decades of centralized economic planning. Increasing dependency marks the economy of the region with heavy imports of consumers commodities from the mainland which in turn virtually make it impossible for the region to carve a path of economic self-reliance (Kishan: 2008). Integration of the economy of the region into the world capitalist system through the mechanics of colonial imperialism led to its transformation into a peripheral underdeveloped economy.

C. MDONER: Ancillary to International Financial Institutions

Baruah and Bandyopadhyay (2005) have very clearly projected the distinction of the Compound Growth Rates of different sectors of GDP at 198—81 price between the North-East and India during 1980-81 to 1997-98 which is illustrated in Table 1.2.

It is apparent from the above data that there has been a steady growth in all the sectors in North-East. However, there existed a wide disparity in the growth rates of all the components of Net State Domestic Product (NSDP) between North East India and the rest of India except for the primary sector. The growth rate of the primary sector in North-East is rather slightly better than the national average. The inequality is most pronounced in the manufacturing sector.

Ministry of Development of North Eastern Region (MDONER)

The Department of Development of North Eastern Region (DONER) was created in September 2001 by an amendment to the Government of India's Allocation of Business Rule. The Department was formally inaugurated on 1st November, 2001. This Department was accorded the status of a Ministry *vide* Gazette notification of Government of India dated 27th May, 2004. The Ministry has the following bodies: NE Development Finance Corp., NE Handicrafts & Handlooms Development Corp., NE Regional Agriculture Marketing Corp., North Eastern Council and Sikkim Mining Corp. in order to implement its policies and programmes. While it is interesting to note that only the NE region has a separate Ministry in India, there are important concerns that are highlighted. First, the creation of a new department for the NE questions the very existence and role of North Eastern Council (NEC) which was constituted as far back as 1971 in order "to act as advisory body in respect of socio-economic development and balanced development of the North Eastern Areas". Further, with DONER being upgraded to a Ministry, the decision-making power for the NE was shifted away from Shillong to *Delhi*. A far more dangerous and disempowering trend is also visible after the creation of the Ministry. Soon after being upgraded to a Ministry, IFIs began their push in the NE (*see Chart* A on IFI Trend). It is natural to ask, whether these IFIs, particularly ADB, had a hand in the creation of this Ministry as a special purpose vehicle to push their designs in the NE. Another trend that is evident is that the Ministry becomes a facilitator for IFIs (and private investors) to auction the region with major decisions shifting beyond even Delhi to IFI headquarters in Manila, Washington DC. and Tokyo. This became more evident when civil society groups who were trying to access documents relating to projects in the NE have to wait for approval from the head offices of these IFIs. This issue needs to be further investigated as it goes to the heart of the question: who controls the future of development in the region?

Source: Ramananda and Yumnam (2006).

Table 1.2: Growth Rate for North-East India and India

Sectors	*Growth Rates for North-East*	*Growth Rates for India*
Agriculture	2.34 (16.85)	2.9 (12.06)
Manufacturing	2.33 (7.22)	6.4 (43.57)
Primary Sector	2.80 (4.12)	2.3 (7.16)
Services	5.20 (44.16)	6.3 (58.39)
Infrastructure	5.79 (28.95)	5.8 (49.85)
NSDP	3.88 (32.49)	5.1 (43.27)

Barua and Bandyopadhyay (2005).

Table 1.3 reveals the Compound Growth Rates of NSDP and per capita NSDP for different States of North-East and India. It is evident that except for Assam, Manipur and Meghalaya, NSDP growth rates are above or close to the national average rate of 5.1 per cent. However, the NSDP growth rate for the major State of the region, Assam, is very dismal. Its growth rate, 3.3 per cent, is far behind the all-India average. The per capita NSDP of the constituent States of the region indicates a dismal picture of disparity in comparison with the all-India average. When India's Gross Domestic Product was growing at an average over 6 per cent in real terms, economies of the region were growing at a lesser rate during 1992-99. NSDP of the seven States of the region has shown a marked decline over the years. Agriculture is the mainstay of North-East and it shows sharp disparity with the rest of the country. There is also a wide disparity of per capita income between North-East India and rest of the country. Per capita income of Assam in 1950-51 was to be 4 per cent above the all-India average. However, it led to a drastic fall showing it at 41 per cent below the national average at 1998-99 current prices and 45 per cent below the all-India average at 1980-81 prices. While per capita income at 1980 prices grew by 40 per cent for all-India during 1980-90, Assam grew by only 20 per cent. When all-India growth rate of per capita was 37 per cent during 1980-1998, in Assam it grew by just 10 per cent. Similar trend was reported for other States of the region during the same period.

Table 1.3: Compound Growth Rates of NSDP and Per Capita NSDP for Different States of North-East and India

NE States	*NSDP Growth Rates*	*Per Capita Growth*	*Population Growth*
Arunachal	8.12 (41.08)	5.20 (27.9)	2.9 (76.17)
Assam	3.31 (28.73)	1.13 (9.62)	2.2 (182.51)
Manipur	4.86 (70.96)	2.38 (32.03)	2.5 (153.32)
Meghalaya	4.97 (22.66)	2.11 (11.31)	2.8 (175.93)
Mizoram	8.31 (14.65)	5.74 (12.14)	3.3 (37.07)
Nagaland	7.28 (25.94)	3.04 (9.74)	4.2 (56.21)
Tripura	6.42 (21.93)	3.67 (11.75)	2.7 (76.87)
NE	3.88 (32.49)	3.33 (33.77)	2.4 (230.84)
India	5.1 (43.27)	3.30 (23.14)	1.8 (13.38)

Baruah and Bandyopadhyay (2005).

Baruah and Bandyopadhyay (*ibid.*) write that there is a possibility that due to the neglect of the Central Government fruits of development have not been evenly distributed across various regions of the country. But it may not be fully true since due to some

Chart 1.1: IFI Funding in N.E.—Existing Projects

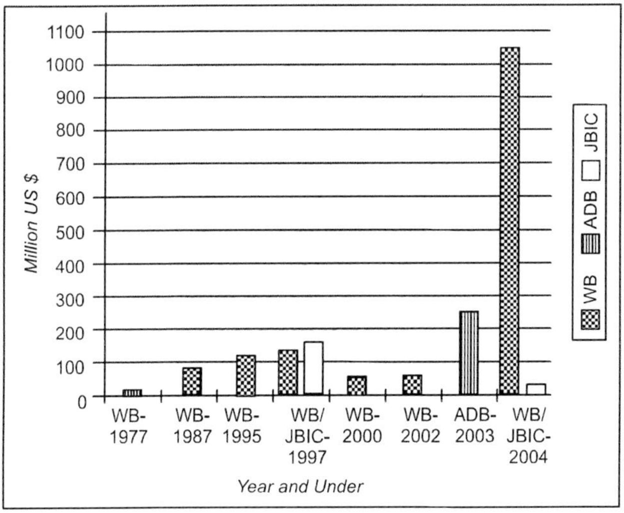

Chart 1.2: IFI Funded Projects in Pipeline

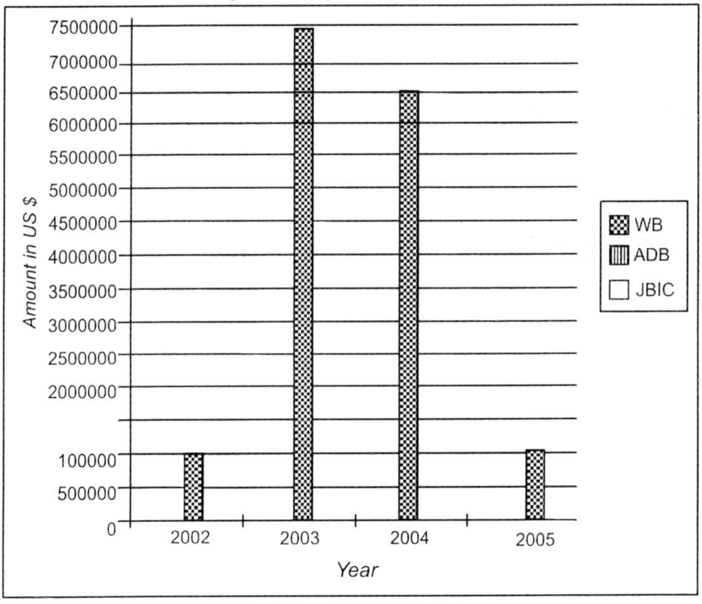

WB = World Bank
ADB = Asian Development Bank
JBIC = Japan Bank of International Co-operation

endogenous factors of the region—unwilling to grow also may lead to uneven development. However, it may not be fully unjustified to state that due to lack of growth of the market (For which the Central Government may be held responsible) the growth rate has remained low in the North-East.

Table 1.4 shows that the inflow of Foreign Direct Investment (FDI) in the North-East is quite meagre as compared to other regions of the country. As a result, the region has not been able to gain the benefits of technology transfer and skill development, consequent due to liberalization of the national economy.

Table 1.4: State-wise Foreign Investment (August 1991 to March 2004)

States	*No. of Approvals*	*Amount of FCI (Rs. Millions)*
Assam	19	14.95
Arunachal	2	110.60
Manipur	2	31.85
Meghalaya	5	529.60
Mizoram	1	15.22
Nagaland	2	36.80
Tripura	4	30.88
Total	35	769.90
All India	25,482	29,23,582.82

Source: North-Eastern Region Vision 2020.

It has been estimated by the Shukla Commission that over rupees 2,500 crore worth of consumer items are imported from mainland India annually. The external dependence of Assam becomes more glaring as the most industrialized State in the region, imports 74 per cent of its milk product, 98 per cent of its meat requirements and 94 per cent of its eggs from outside the region. In spite, of adequate rainfall and natural abundance of water resources, the State imports half of its fish requirements from outside. Similarly, Manipur which produces a variety of fishes traditionally is presently compelled to import three-fourth of its requirements from Andhra Pradesh. Manipur also imports chicks and fowl feed from far-off States like Andhra Pradesh, Orissa and West Bengal. Consequently, its local entrepreneurs are never able to compete. Transformation of the region into a market for manufactured goods from mainland India went hand in hand with increasing underdevelopment in spite of sheer abundance of prime resources like oil, timber, tea, coal, limestone and other forest resources. While very large amount of crude oil is drilled from the oilfields in Assam, only a small part of it is refined in the State and the most part (33 lakh tonnes) is refined at Barauni in the State of Bihar. The exploitation of the Centre becomes all the more revealing as one finds that while Assam receives only Rs. 632 royalty for per tonne oil, the Centre earns an average dividend of Rs. 2623 per tonne.

The tea industry has also been a major source of exploitation in the North-East. The number of tea estates in Assam increased from 785 in 1951 to 848 tea estates in 1993. The area covered by tea estates also rose from 1,55,674 hectares to 2,36,811 hectares during the same period. Figures indicate that Assam produced an average of 250 million kgs. Annually during 1962 to 1999 at an international price estimate of 2.5 US billion dollars. However, the tea companies, most of which are owned by outsiders, have invested almost nothing in the State from the huge profits generated. The forest wealth of North-East has also been exploited ruthlessly in the interest of the States outside. The nature of ruthless plundering and exploitation can be comprehended by the virtual absence of any substantial forest based industry in the region except for the odd miniscule saw mills and a few paper mills in Assam. Timber from the region feed the plywood industries in West Bengal, Delhi, Uttar Pradesh, Haryana, etc.

Many of the Constitutional laws/Acts themselves had led to direct exclusion of the North-East region. The verdicts of Hon'ble Justice Kripal and Hon'ble Justice Verma stand to be a good illustration of this. The December 12, 1996 Supreme Court judgement banning felling of trees in all categories of forests in the North-East and transportation of wood based products within the region except for defence and government requirements too became a subject of acrimony to the indigenous peoples. In the absence of any major technical industry, timber is a major source of income to the villagers of the region. But the judgement deprived them of this source of income as well in the name of environment (Nongbri: 2001). Many were peeved as to why the Hon'ble Court did not deem it to be equally applicable in other parts of the country. The onus of forest preservation does not lie only on the people of North-East.

D. Police Control and Denial of Civil Liberties

Very often it is realized that India was not a nation-state as we find at present, from the ancient days. It became so only since 1947. Prior to that, it was a British colony. But on attaining independence all the States did not join it automatically, particularly so in the case of North-East. Mukhim (2006) writes, "When India became free, the various tribes of the North Eastern region were made to sign the Instrument of Accession into the Indian Union, by coercion, in many instances by using devious and dubious methods. After the British left this sub-continent, people were not consulted or given a free and a clear choice to chart their future course of action. While it is true that freedom was won intrinsically by the blood, sweat and tears of people like Gandhi, Nehru and Tilak *et al.* and that the people of North-East frontiers had a peripheral engagement, to assume that the people of a particular race should be willing to be subsumed under another emerging nation is presumptuous. It is but natural that freedom from British rule was seen as a mere exchange of masters. The perception remains that India, with its sheer might, has co-opted all smaller independent principalities unto itself". Not surprisingly, in the entire North-East there is a sense of disgruntlement and ethnic upsurge being common to all the States, violence is widespread.

Das and Verma (2003) have noted that the main aim of the British in establishing the Police and formulating criminal laws was the subjugation of the Indian people (cited in Subramanian: 2007). The Central Police Forces (CPF) become almost permanent fixtures in "disturbed areas" such as Jammu and Kashmir, the North-Eastern States and the central tribal belt affected by Naxalite activities. The CPFs and the Intelligence Bureau (IB) are thus the key Central Police Officers (CPOs) in public order management in large parts of the country on a daily basis, despite the Constitutional stipulation that 'law and order' and police are State subjects. The massive growth of Central Police Forces (CPFs) after independence may be said to underscore two developments: (i) The gradual centralization of internal security planning and action; (ii) The increasing reliance on the instrument of force to solve conflict (Subramanian: *ibid.,* 2007).

In the entire North-Eastern States control over the law and order and general people, is much more stringent. Not surprisingly, the presence of the security forces is very high as compared to other parts of the country. While the national average for the number of police per lakh population in 2003 was 120, it was significantly higher in all the States of the region. Surprisingly, while Mizoram is considered to be one of the most peaceful States in the region, it had the highest police presence—770 per one lakh population. While there were 41.4 police per sq km in the country in 1993, Tripura had 161 and Nagaland had 71. At present, there are more than 55,000 armed personnel of the central security forces stationed in the Manipur State. The State has over 14,000 police personnel. Taking into account of the total population of the State, there is one armed personnel for every 20 citizen (HRW 2008).

Table 1.5: Strength of Police Force in NER (2003)

States	*Police per 100 sq. km.*	*Police per lakh of Population*
Arunachal	6.8	510
Assam	66.4	190
Manipur	61.3	550
Meghalaya	38.7	360
Mizoram	33.7	770
Nagaland	71	570
Sikkim	43.8	550
Tripura	161	510
India	41.4	120

Source: North Eastern Region Vision 2020.

There are at least three main aspects of structural violence in the North-Eastern region of India. These are: (i) the massive presence of so-called security forces, which prevents the civilian State governments from functioning normally; (ii) the powerlessness of the law courts in the region to bring the security forces to account for abuses, which is exacerbated by procrastination and subservience to the political authority of the central courts; and (iii) the virtual absence of any practical application of human rights agreements (Parratt, 2005). Figure 1.1 indicates only the security camps of Inspector General Assam Rifles (IGAR)—South Camps in Manipur, besides IGAR, there are many central security forces deployed under the banner 57th Mountain Division: (i) 59th Mountain brigade—(at Churachandpur): 19 Rajput Regiment, 9 Raj Rifles; (ii) 73 Mountain Brigade—(at Bishnupur): 11 Garhwal Rifles, 5/8 Gorkha Rifles, 12 Grenadiers 10 AR; (iii) 44 Mountain Brigade—(at Chakpikarong): 7 Sikh Light Infantry, 27 Madras Regiment, 9 Rajput Regiment; (iv) 26 Sector Assam Rifles (AR)—(at Chandel): 16 AR, 36AR, 37 AR, 24 AR, 18 AR, 33 AR; (v) 57 Mountain Artillery—(at Haflong): 9 Para Regiment, 26 AR Medium Regiment. In addition to this, there is an independent Operation (Army) based at Leimakhong, Special Force-Para Troopers, 10 Battalions of Central Reserve Police Force

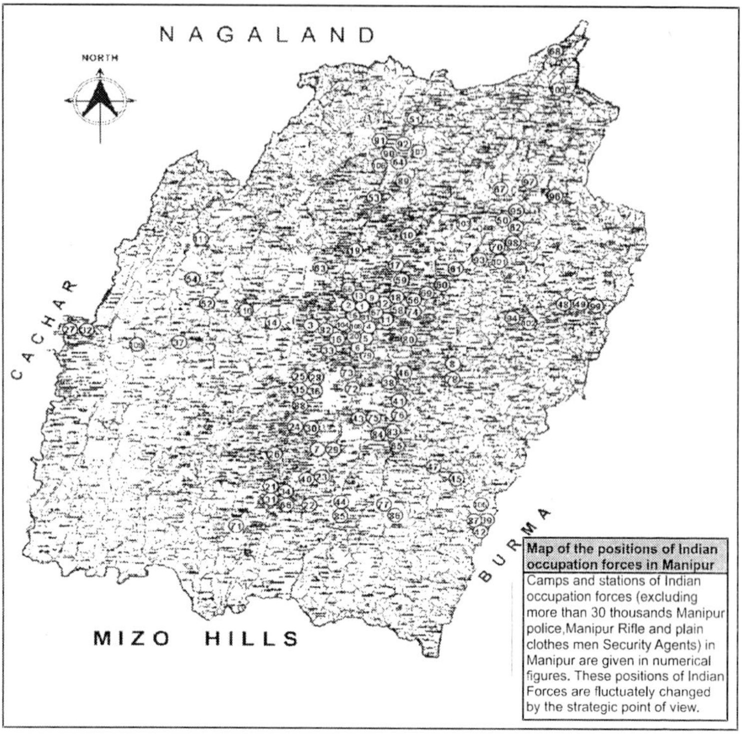

Fig. 1.1: Deployment of Central Security Forces in Manipur (till 1996)

Note: Map showing the location of Indian military forces in Manipur—each number represents the location of a base or a battalion. Notice the concentration in the centre of the country, suggesting an occupying regime rather than defence of the border.

Source: Robinson, Andrew 2005.

(CRPF) under one Inspector General, Two Battalions of Border Security Forces (BSF), Indian Reserve Battalions (IRB) (Human Rights Initiatives 2009 and Centre for Organisation Research and Education, Manipur, 2007). These immense armed forces are, it is argued, required to control a population of just over two million population of Manipur.

Many draconian Acts have been promulgated to control the political upheavals in North Eastern India. National Security Act (NSA) and Unlawful Activities (Prevention) Act are some of them. But one of the worst among them is the Armed Forces Special Powers

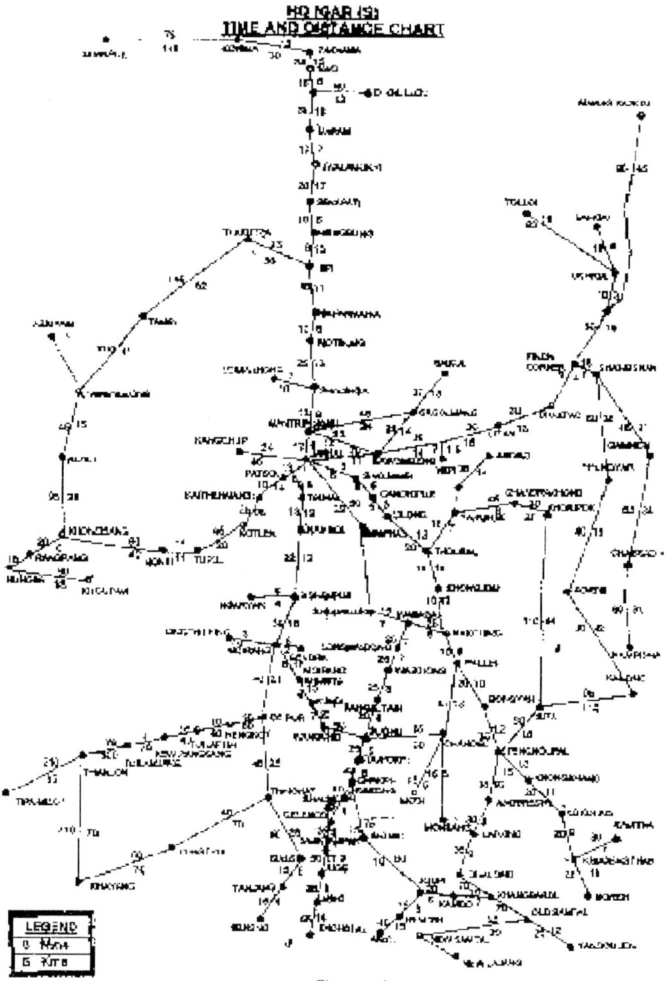

Figure 6

Source: *Justice First*, December 2008, Vol. I, No. 1.

Figure 1.2: Military Installation Only for Inspector General Assam Rifles (IGAR)-South in Manipur.

Act (AFSPA) 1958. B.K. Roy Burman (*n.d.*) writes, "Under the leadership of Gandhi and Nehru the politics of Indian nationalism tended to a certain extent to be the politics of global humanism. But in free India, not to speak of global humanism, even the humanist concern for the country, as a whole seems to have been eroded, particularly among the political class. Politics has degenerated into a calculus of power. The AFSPA's predecessor—the Armed Force Special Power Ordinance 1942, has been enacted in order to neutralize Quit India Movement by the British colonialist. It was a colonial instrument, used for legitimization and continuation of colonialism. The AFSPA 1958 of India inherited the same powerful political potency. The AFSPA in 1958 has been enacted in order to quell the Naga uprising in the Naga Hills in Assam. After four decades, like a nuclear chain reaction, the law has been amended a number of times to accommodate changes in the names and the number of States. It now applies to all of North-East India either partially or fully. It is the most dehumanized manifestation of the obsession with power in the name of State security, to the complete indifference about human security. Army officers have legal immunity for their actions. There can be no prosecution, suit or any other legal proceeding against anyone acting under that law. Nor is the government's judgement on why an area is found to be 'disturbed' subject to judicial review. It is Invocation of Unproclaimed Emergency. The Act empowers an army officer (even non-commissioned) in an area that is proclaimed as "disturbed", to:

4. Any commissioned officer, warrant officer, non-commissioned officer or any other person of equivalent rank in the Armed Forces may, in a disturbed area—
   (a) if he is of the opinion that it is necessary to do so for maintenance of public order, after giving such due warning as he may consider necessary, fire upon or otherwise use force, even to the causing of death, against any person who is acting in contravention of any law or order for the time being in the disturbed area prohibiting the assembly of five or more persons or the carrying of weapons or of things capable of being used as weapons or firearms, ammunition or explosive substances;
   (b) if he is of the opinion that it is necessary to do so, destroy any armed dump, prepared or fortified position or shelter from which armed attacks are made or are likely to be made, or any structure used as a training camp for armed volunteers or utilized as a hideout by armed gangs or absconders wanted for any offence;
   (c) arrest without warrant, any person who has committed a cognisable offence or against whom a reasonable

suspicion exist that he has committed or is about to commit a cognisable offence and may use such force as may be necessary to effect the arrest;

(d) enter and search without warrant any premises to make any such arrest as aforesaid or to recover any person believed to be wrongfully restrained or confined or any property or any arms, ammunition or explosive substances believed to be unlawfully kept in such premises; and may for that purpose use force as may be necessary.

5. Any person arrested and taken into custody under this Act shall be made over to the officer in charge of the nearest police station with the least possible delay, together with a report of the circumstances occasioning the arrest.
6. No prosecution, suit or other legal proceeding shall be instituted, except with the previous sanction of the Central Government against any person in respect of anything done or purported to be done in exercise of powers conferred by this Act.

The roots of the AFSPA can be traced with the infamous Rowlatt Act 1919. The passing of Rowlatt Act was similar to that of the AFSPA 1958, in the sense that every non-official British Indian citizen was against the Act. People of British India under the leadership of Gandhi opposed the Act by organizing a *satyagraha.* The Act authorized the government to arrest any person without trial, to intern and restrict movement of persons suspected of anti-British activities. The Act enabled the British Government to suspend the rights of *habeas corpus*, which is the foundation of civil liberties in any society. The judges were empowered to try political cases without jury. No appeal against their decisions was possible. Mere possession of an incriminating document was made punishable. People who protested against the Act on 13th April, 1919 at Jallianwalla Bagh were massacred by a body of troops under General Dyer. Thus, was formed the seminal entity called lawlessness in the guise of law, also called Rowlatt Act (Singh Lokendrajit: 2004).

In spite of referring the Bill to a Joint Parliamentary Committee to examine the statute and discussing the same in details, on 18th August, 1958, the AFSPA has been adopted after two hours, long summary debate by the Parliament. Manipur MP Sri L. Achou Singh urged against the bill, "*this is a black law....How can we imagine that these military officers should be allowed to shoot to kill and without warrant arrest and search? This is lawless Law*". Manipur Hill MP Rungsung Suisa argued against the AFSPA, "*All these Ordinances and sending of armed forces will not solve the problem*". MP Sri Warrior (Trichur) opposed the bill, "*the whole of Assam and Manipur is going to come under Martial Law though Martial Law and emergency are not declared*". In the same vein, MP Sri Mahanty opposed, "*what I am trying to submit is that this is Martial Law*" he further argued. "*But we don't want a free India with barbed wires and concentration camps, where a havaldar can shoot at sight any man*". Many MPs opposed the Bill as the invocation of unproclaimed emergency through the backdoor. However, the brute majority of the ruling Congress got the Bill passed without any elaborate debate in Parliament in just 2 hours (cited in Sanajaoba: 2006).

Singh Lokendrajit (2004) observed that the Section 2 (b) of the Act defines a 'disturbed area' in an area which is for the time being declared by Notification under Section 3 to be disturbed area. Thus, the Central Act defines a disturbed area tautologically. But it is questionable on what ground the area is declared (disturbed) area. What are the criteria, or are there any social parameters that can be the basis of forming opinion. What is the definition or concept of 'disturbed' by using which the Central Government or the State Government is to form opinion on whether an area is disturbed? According to the Hon'ble Supreme Court, the area to be declared disturbed must be internally so disturbed so as to necessitate deployment of the Union army in aid of State civil administration. On the nature of this internal disturbance, the Hon'ble Supreme Court in its landmark judgement observes that:

> There is no material on the record to show that the disturbed conditions in the States to which the Central Act has been extended are due to an armed rebellion. Even if the disturbance is as a result of armed rebellion by a section of the people in those States the disturbances may not be of such a magnitude as to pose a threat to the security of the country or a part thereof so as to call for invocation of the emergency power 352. If the disturbances caused by armed rebellion does not pose a threat to the security of the country and the situation can be handled by deployment of armed forces of the Union in the disturbed area, there appears to

> be no reason why the drastic power under Article 352 should be invoked. It is, therefore, not possible to hold that the Central Act, which is primarily enacted to confer certain powers on armed forces when deployed in aid of civil power to deal with the situation of internal disturbances in a disturbed area, has been enacted to deal with a situation which can only be dealt with by issuing a proclamation of emergency under Article 352.

The sum and substance is clear enough. Internal disturbance which need not even armed rebellion, not good enough for invoking Emergency provisions, but sound enough to invite deployment of Union force. There is not a single trace or suggestion as to what objective conditions constitute this 'soundness' in the hallow body of AFSPA. Just as beauty lies in the eye of the beholder, the soundness of deploying Union forces lies in the eye of the Union or State Government. So, ultimately, a disturbed area is an area which has been declared a disturbed area. Nothing more nothing less! What an oppressive tautology! What arbitrariness! What political expediency!

On the contrary, G.B. Pant—the then Home Minister, while introducing AFSPA on August 18, 1958 said that certain misguided sections of the Naga in Assam and Manipur were indulging in arson, murder, loot, dacoity, etc., and that it had become necessary to adopt effective measures for the protection of the people in those areas and that to enable the armed forces to handle the situation effectively, it had been considered necessary to enact legislation. If "arson, murder, loot, dacoity, etc.", are the yardsticks for the imposition of the AFSPA, then the Act has been imposed discriminatorily in the North-East States. There has been equal number of such incidents, if not more in for instance, Uttar Pradesh and Bihar, where incidents of violence and insecurity of common citizenry have been outrageous, systematic and persistent. Armed insurrections have taken place also in other parts of India, for instance, by the Maoist Communist Centre in Bihar and by Naxalites in Bihar, Andhra Pradesh, West Bengal and Madhya Pradesh. Members of the Shiv Sena in Maharashtra have resorted to "arson, murder, loot, dacoity, etc.", during communal riots in India. The most recent situation in Gujarat exemplifies such situations in other parts of India (Centre for Organization Education and Research 2002; hereafter CORE).

AFSPA is presented as an instrument '*in aid of civil power*' (Section 3 of the Act) to '*suppress*' '*armed revolt*' or '*armed insurgency'* in the North-East. And it was supposed to be a *'temporary measure'*. But over four decades of its existence has shown up all the stated claims (*'in aid of civil power', 'suppression' of 'armed revolt' or 'armed insurgency' and 'temporary measure'*) as false. This begs the question: What has the military been doing all these decades and how has AFSPA furthered counter-insurgency? Such questions, along with subversion of democratic institutions and principles through prolonged and continuous deployment of the armed forces under AFSPA, raise questions of militarism. The Act is an act of legitimizing the involvement of the military in the domestic space, and that it does not supplement but supplant the *'civil power'* (Akoijam & Tarun: 2005). The AFSPA is so to speak a measure of "order" more than of "law"; although it is supposedly a legal measure itself, it in fact legitimates the otherwise extra-legal brutalities of the occupying army, granting these atrocities both legal impunity and a discursive legitimation in the form of the "war on terror" (Robinson: 2005). While in Jammu and Kashmir, AFSPA operate to apprehend *"terrorists" or "militants"* but in the North-East, quite contrary to the earlier application, the powers are used to *"maintain law and order"*. In addition the GOI relies on the police during the movement of DMK and the communist while depends on the army for the Nagas (Chasie and Hazarika: 2009) in particular and North-East in general as well as Kashmir.

North Eastern India is lamenting the 50 years of suffering under the AFSPA in spite of enjoying 62 years of independence and democracy. In spite of the criticism and recommendation from Government of India committee namely: (a) Justice Jeevan Reddy Report (2005); (b) Administrative Reforms Committee by Vedrabha Moily (2007); (c) Working Groups on Confidence Building Measures in Jammu and Kashmir headed by Mohammad Hamid Ansari (2007); and International: (a) UN Human Rights Committee 1997; (b) UN Special Rapporteurs on Extrajudicial, Summary or Arbitrary Executions, 2006; (c) Committee on Elimination of Displacement Against Women; 2007, Committee on Elimination of Racial Discrimination 2007, to repeal the Act. The Government of India is silent over it citing the Act is necessary for national security. The concept of "National Unity" is in many instances used by the authoritarian governments to justify repression of divergent opinions and to cling on to power rather than to try to find constructive solutions that take on board the voices of indigenous peoples (Jensen: 2001).

Besides AFSPA, Prevention of Unlawful Activities Act 1967, Punjab Security Act 1953, Terrorists and Disruptive Activities Prevention Act, 1985 (now repeal) and National Security Act, etc., are imposed in North Eastern States. This Act and its procedure are arguably *ultra vires* of various key articles of the Constitution of India, including the fundamental rights. It also violates the International legislation like the International Covenant on Civil and Political Rights (ICCPR) and International Covenant on Economic, Social and Cultural Rights (ICESCR), which India is a signatory member. But the security establishment and politicians had dismissed the reports (Chenoy: 1999).

In Nagaland the ethnic strife is continuing almost right from the time of independence. The Naga did not accept the imposition of Indian rule after the departure of the British and have been involved in armed struggle after the peaceful means failed to produce any result. The Constitution of India too has been using brutal coercive measures to quell the situation. The situation right now is to some extent better with the declaration of cease fire by both the Naga underground and the Government of India as well.

When the Assam Rifles outpost was captured by the MNF in Aizwal—the State capital of Mizoram, it was bombed by the Indian Air Force to create panic among the masses. The Mizos of Mizoram too had revolted against the Indian state in the 1960s to 1980s. As a measure of 'counter insurgency' the security forces regrouped majority of the interior villages and created resettlements by the roadside under the euphemism of "People's Progressive Village" (P.P.V). 516 villages were regrouped into 110 grouping centres affecting more than 70,000 lives. Grouping of villages severely affected the traditional '*Jhum*' cultivation or shifting hill cultivation. Curfew used to be imposed between dusk to dawn and people were given work permits to go to fields only during the day time. This severely affected the crop output as many people gave up cultivation. The rice production fell from 75,000 tonnes to 35,000 tonnes a year between 1967 to 1972 (Rangaswami: 1978). These affected the social harmony in most villages. There was a rapid rise in crimes like gambling and murder (Nunthara: 1981). In every Group centre, the democratic institutions were virtually withdrawn and administration was initially left to military Post Commanders. Subsequently, Administrative Officers were appointed. Although the Mizos were quite fed up with herding them into concentration camps, very few dared to resist openly (Lalrintluanga: 2009).

The racial divide is quite stark in matters of security arrangement. One senior Police Officer from the 'mainstream India' who was an advisor to the Governor of Manipur recommended that in order to stop penetration of the government departments by local militants, battalions of Central Reserve Police Force (CRPF) should guard all government offices and the residential neighbourhoods housing Central and State Government officials. Furthermore, he recommended that ten battalions of the Central Para-Military Force (CPMF) be deployed in the Manipur valley in a "counter-insurgency grid" (Baruah: 2006). Such racial high handedness has been reported by Sanjay Barbora as well (Barbora: 2005). He states that in the year 2000 when the members of United Peoples Democratic Front—an ethnic militia comprising of Karbi youth—attacked Hindi speaking agriculturists (Encroachers—outsiders from the Hindi belt) in the Hamren sub-division of Karbi Anglong district in Assam, the settlers armed and aided by the CRPF, attacked Karbi villages, looting and killing many Karbi farmers in retaliation. Along with the increase of central security forces, the human rights violation in the State also increased which is committed in the name of counter-insurgency operation. It is mainly because the Indian State largely relies on police machinery not only for information pertaining to social conflict and violence, but also for the analysis and interpretation of the phenomena of violence in terms of their nature, causes and solution that the political problem is construed as a problem of law and order (Subramanian: 2007).

Akoijam and Tarunkumar (2005) observed that American troops deployed and engaged in actual combat in the recent Iraq war primarily came from the American soil, not from its military bases in foreign countries. In this sense, the 'American network of (military) bases is not a sign of military preparedness but of militarism'. In a similar sense, continuous enforcement of AFSPA and deployment of troops under the Act seem to serve as a reminder of a *'presence'* rather than *'combating'* the insurgency *per se* in the region. This reminder is also communicated in frightening dimensions by the so-called 'excesses' in which men; women and children are killed in *'retaliation'* to attacks on the 'armed forces' by the *'insurgents'*. More than being cases of *'human rights abuses'*, those *'excesses'* for which no accountability can be fixed on anybody are reminders of the militarism that has subverted the democratic institutions and ethos in the North-East. The concentration of security forces in the valley of

Manipur is such that Andrew Robinson remarks it as an occupational force rather than the defence of the country (Robinson: 2005).

The Indian State justification for deploying military in domestic space is that, the State police being ill equipped to handle militancy, defence forces have to be deployed to assist the State police. Yet the defence forces do not wish to operate within the purview of the civil laws and legal code of conduct. This amounts to saying that the military is above the people/citizen. What is inevitable is that since the military operates at different plane with extra civil and constitutional safeguards, violation of civil and human rights are something that is bound to happen. Further, closing down to the citizen any possible legal protection and accountability against the defence forces unless allowed by the Central Government, as marked in the provision under AFSPA, clearly shows the martial law in domestic space (Oinam, 2008). There is an overwhelming sense of unease and fearfulness, which disrupts normal social and business life, in which the security forces are seen not as agents of security and peace, but rather as agents of an oppressive psychological and physical pressure which makes normal human life all but impossible (Parratt: 2005). Unrest of fake encounter, deprivation of right to live, cultural assimilation, distortion, baffled education, unemployment psyche-ailment, economic disparaging and of globalization, is continually haunting our society on all front. All are living under the shadow of unpredictable moments of fearsomeness. People are living quite insecured lives with so-called security personnel as well with insurgent groups. Though the fact is that people living in a land of law should be secured by the government, the present reality is that the government is by degree, acting against people aspiration. Armed Forces Special Powers Act 1958 and its counter-products, fear psychosis of the people have proven it (Bhubol: 2009).

E. Migration and Land Alienation

Migration has been a major problem acting as an impediment to the development process in the North-East. As it is the region has a long and porous international border whereby millions of people across the borders have been regularly sneaking into the region. This has been causing not only economic problems for the indigenous peoples but also resulting into a skewed demographic order and thereby drastically reducing the ratio of the local people *vis-à-vis* the migrants.

The situation has further deteriorated due to immigration of labour force and business community from the 'mainland' India. In many of the North-East States the migrants start dominating over the indigenous peoples, like it happened in the case of Tripura and Sikkim. The indigenous tribes in these two States have been thoroughly decimated due to massive migrations from across the international borders. Today they have become a hapless minority. This could happen only because of the deliberate policies of the governments and their lacklustre attitude to the entire issue. One of the proposals for nationalising space in the North-East especially Arunachal made after the China war was just such a strategy of nation-building through forced migration. One opposition Indian politician even proposed that 1,00,000 farmers from Punjab be settled in North Eastern Frontier Agency (Arunachal) in order to assimilate into India (Guha cited in Baruah: 2005). A Nepali Scholar from North East Hill University (NEHU), Shillong also suggested settling down Nepalese ex-army men in Arunachal Pradesh in order to strengthen the process of national integration of the region. This would mean an explicit policy of marginalizing the tribal peoples in their own habitats and, in effect, dismantling the institutions of tribal autonomy established in colonial times and modified and reinforced by the Constitution's Sixth Schedule (Baruah: 2005).

The bleak situation can be gauged by the fact that while the decadal growth rate for India between 1991 and 2001 was 21.54 per cent it was 25.29 per cent for the North-East. In Nagaland, the decadal growth during the same period was 64.52 per cent. The entire North-East region has witnessed tremendous amount of migration from outside the region—from different parts of India as well as outside India. The refugee problem and illegal Bangladeshi immigrant problem has been witnessed in the entire region and more so in the State of Assam. In Tripura 6,09,998 Bengali refugees from erstwhile East Pakistan were settled and rehabilitated between 1967 to 1971. This caused enormous problem of land alienation to the local tribals. In 1951, cultivators constituted 62.94 per cent of the total tribal workforce in the State, while only 8.93 per cent was in the category of agricultural labourers. But in 1981, only 43.57 per cent of the tribal workforce was cultivators and the number of agricultural labourers had risen to 23.91 per cent. In 2001, the percentage of cultivators in Tripura was only 31.6 per cent. In Manipur, the number of migrants (7,04,488—30.71%) with their offspring outnumber the

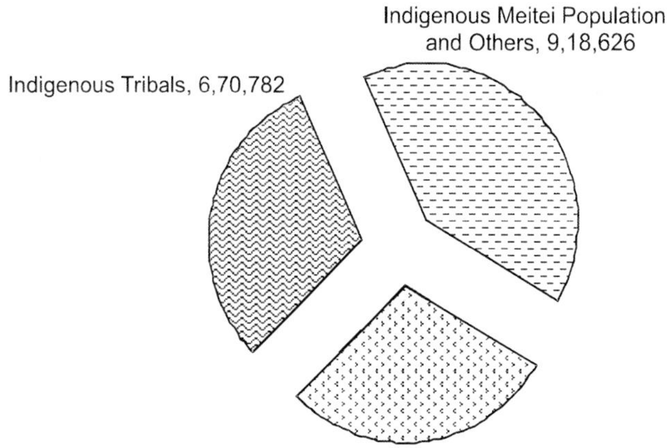

Fig. 1.3: Population Composition of Manipur (Estimated for 2001).
Source: United Committee Manipur 2005.

indigenous tribal population (6,70,782—29.24%) of the State (United Committee, Manipur: 2005).

The Government of India had recently decided to construct 145 mega dams to tap the hydroelectric potential of the region to convert the North-East into India's power house (Hussain: 2008). This has encouraged large-scale migrations from outside the region. A large fleet of construction workers can be seen all around the region. In Arunachal Pradesh, there is not only a demographic marginalization taking place but there is also a massive amount of *benami* transactions of land transpiring. Extraction of natural resources from the State to outside is also rampant. 30 years back in Arunachal Pradesh, the percentage of Scheduled Tribes (ST) population was more than 80 per cent; it had been reduced to 64.2 per cent in 2001. The percentage of ST population in the urban areas is as low as 43.4 per cent. In Tawang district where there has been a substantial Nepalese migration, the percentage of ST population is just around 29 per cent in the urban areas. Lohit district has only 38 per cent ST population. In the urban areas of Lohit district, the ST population is just 19.8 per cent. The outside migration in Lohit is confirmed by the fact that it shows a sex ratio of 829 while it is 1,003 for the entire State of Arunachal Pradesh. There seems to have been a lot of outside male migration into the district. The main apparent benefit of the proposed projects, namely power, is not meant for the North-East region, but for the rest of the region. For if the existing (installed capacity being 1,790 MW) and under construction projects (with installed capacity of 1,545 MW) in the region are taken into consideration, they have enough capacity, if operated optimally, to satisfy power needs of the region for at least another decades if not two. Parliamentary Standing Committee on energy in its report for the last year has noted that even peak demand in the region is only 926 MW. The officials of NEEPCO and NEC admit that the new big dam projects are not required for the region. The Central Government and its institutions like NEEPCO, NPHC and Brahmaputra Board, and Water and Power Ministries are taking the decisions for the region, with practically no involvement of the people of the region. But the social and environmental costs would be borne by the people of the region (Thakkar: 2005).

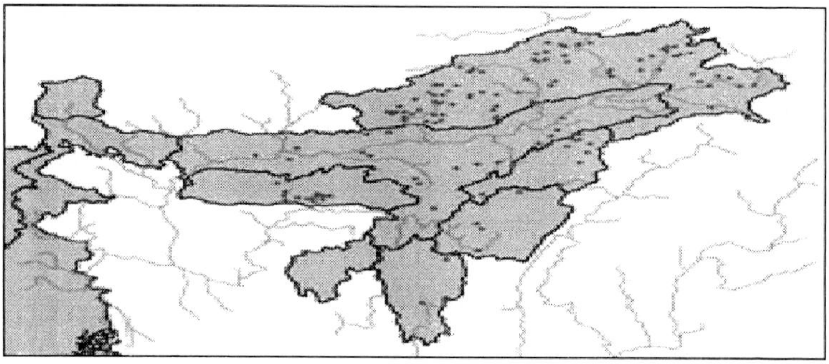

Fig. 1.4: Proposed Dams for India's North-East excluding Sikkim.

Source: Vagholikar, 2007

Increasing pressure on land as a result of population growth compounded by quantum leap through massive influx of immigrants from Bihar, Uttar Pradesh, Orissa, Rajasthan, Punjab, Bangladesh and Nepal and recent trends in the wake of globalization triggered liberalization transforming cultivation configurations from basic crops to cash crops contributing to significant increase in dependency. Increasing trends of displacement or rural cultivators as a result of haphazard urbanization without concomitant creation of productive base have been widely noticed. Studies on the primary level of economy reveal that an agriculturally surplus generating State like Manipur has turned into an importer of rice and other foodgrains ever since the merger with India in the post-British period (Table 1.6). 20 per cent of its requirement is imported from mainland India.

Table 1.6: Area, Production and Rice Surplus in Manipur Valley (1891-1941)

Year	*Population (Valley)*	*Area (Tonnes)*	*Demand (Tonnes)*	*Rice Production (Tonnes)*	*Surplus (Tonnes)*	*Per cent Surplus*
1891	1,35,782	26,500	28,107	38,160	10,053	26
1901	1,91,207	42,283	39,580	60,755	21,175	35
1931	2,86,843	71,316	59,376	1,02,695	43,319	42
1941	3,43,694	75,370	71,145	1,08,533	37,388	34

Source: Priyoranjan, 2005.

F. Developmental Indicators

The development indicators should broadly indicate the pattern of rural and urban development, resource mobilization, quality of life, social integration, social stratification and mobility and participation of different categories of the population in the developmental process. These should also include the distribution of development benefits in space and time and also among the diverse social strata and groups and communities (Roy Burman, B.K.: 2000). Failure of economic policies and packages in the North-East can be perceived strikingly clear from a cursory glance at some of the basic indices commonly used to measure the state of economic and social development.

Communication

Communication infrastructure is extremely poor in the North-East. The water transport facilities through Brahmaputra river and Barak river which existed during the British period has completely degenerated now as there is hardly any commodity flow between India and Bangladesh. The riverine trade is almost totally confined within the North-East region. The print and electronic media too is virtually left out of vision for the citizens of other parts of the country.

Roadways

There has been some improvement in the roadways in the region in the post-independence period, but the roads cutting across the international borders are not much in use. In any case, the facilities are in no way comparable to the country as a whole. The road length per 100 sq km of area shows that it is lower than the national average (74.73) in the States of Assam (114.09), Nagaland (126.79) and Tripura (155.41). But the road length per lakh population is much higher in all the North Eastern States. This is due to comparatively low density of population in the region.

Railways

While rail route km per lakh of population for Assam is 9.5, the national average is 135.6. There is hardly any presence of railways in the other States of North-East. There has virtually been no expansion of the route km per 1,000 sq km between 2001 and 2005 in all the States of North-East except for Tripura (4.3 km to 6.1 km). In fact, there has been a slight fall in the Assam figure (32.1 to 32). The national average went up from 700.4 to 709.9 during the same period. The railways on most of the routes are only single tracked. Most tracks are also just Metre Gauge. While Assam has a length of 1227.7 km Broad Gauge tracks, Nagaland has 11.13 BG. Other States have none.

Power

Power situation in the North-East is quite poor compared to the country as a whole. While in Nagaland the per capita power consumption is 61.4 kwh, the national average is 373 kwh. Only in Meghalaya it is 300.8 kwh.

Telecom

The telecommunication facilities in the North-East are much worse compared to other States of the country. Except for Arunachal Pradesh and Mizoram the teledensity was much lower in the other States in 2001. It was 1.29 in Manipur, 1.55 in Assam, 1.80 in Nagaland, 2.00 in Tripura while the national average was 3.95. The situation did not improve any in December 2004. While the national average went up to 7.02, in Mizoram it grew to 7.13. In all other States, including Arunachal Pradesh it remained much lower than the national figure, 2.41 in Manipur, 2.98 in Nagaland, 2.95 in Tripura. The internet facility too is much poorer in the North-East as compared to other regions. In 2003, Meghalaya, the leading State of the region revealed 212.34 density per lakh population, the national average was 3,260.78. The lowest is Tripura with 36.16 followed by Manipur with 42.59.

Habitation

In the rural areas of North-East usually the villages are neat and clean from outside, but there are few pucca houses. Most people live in kutcha houses and permit the animals to enter inside. Except for Mizoram (52.84%) all the other States revealed in 2001 that very few lived in pucca houses. The national average was 51.62 per cent in 2001. In 2001 only in Sikkim there were few people residing in kutcha houses (16.07%) as compared to the national average of 18.24. 61.6 per cent of the people in Arunachal Pradesh were residing in kutcha houses in the same year. In Mizoram the number of pucca houses are relatively higher due to the process of artificial urbanization which occurred consequent to regrouping of villages as counter-insurgency measure.

The electricity position in the North-East appears to be relatively better and the percentage of households having electric connections was quite high in 2001. But the situation was strikingly poor in the most populated and comparatively more developed States like Assam. While the figure for national average was 55.9 in 2001, it was only 42.7 in Assam. This is not a very positive indication for the region as a whole. It may be construed that power position is not very good in a State which has the best potential for industrial growth owing to the landscape and available skill and manpower. The consumption of electricity in the region all through since 1990-91 has been considerably less than India as a whole. While for Sikkim the record was 1992.4 (The highest for North-East) in 1999-2000, the national average was 354.7 during the same period.

Urbanization

There has been a slow urban growth in the North-East but the rate is lower than the national average except for Mizoram and Arunachal Pradesh. But it is surprising that of late in Manipur there has been some fall in the urban percentage. While in 1981 and 1991 it had a higher percentage of urban population than the national average it became lesser than that in 2001. It appears that either there has been a large number of migration from the urban areas to the rural areas or there may have occurred large migration to the rural areas from outside the State. Other than this, there is a possibility that some of the urban pockets have been brought under the administration of rural areas. In the case of Mizoram, almost 50 per cent of the population dwell in urban areas—(Second highest for all States in India). This has been possible mainly due to the 'grouping' of villages in the 1960s as a counter-insurgency measure. However, these centres are highly parasitic without any sound economic base.

Economy

Table 1.7 indicates that the C/D ratio in North-East India is gradually improving over the years as compared to the all-India scenario. But the data is not very encouraging for Assam, the most populated State in the region. The NER is said to be overdependent on Central resources, but the C/D ratios suggest that there is a net outflow of financial resources from the region. Table 1.8 confirms this pattern a bit more.

From Table 1.8 it is clearly evident that in the entire NER C/D ratio is very much unfavourable. While in most of the States in the region the situation is improving over the years, in the case of Manipur the position has rather gone down between 1997-1998 to 2004-2005. It has receded from 59 to 45 over the years. In Assam, the situation has remained virtually stagnant. In any case the situation is much worse in NER as compared to the all-India figure.

Table 1.7: Trends of Bank Credit-Deposit Ratio of Public Sector Banks and Disbursement by the All-India Financial Institutions

States	*Credit-Deposit Ratio*		*Cumulative Disbursement till March 2003 (Rs. Crore)*
	June 1969	*June 2003*	
Assam	0.39	0.32	1984.9
Arunachal	N.A.	0.16	72.6
Manipur	0.14	0.31	133.9
Meghalaya	0.28	0.27	189.4
Mizoram	N.A.	0.34	76.2
Nagaland	0.06	0.16	78.4
Tripura	0.04	0.24	311.0
All India	0.78	0.54	5,70,254.3

Source: *Dialogue*, Vol. 10, No. 3.

Table 1.8 Credit-Deposit Ratio of SCBs in the North-East Region

States	*1997-08*	*1998-99*	*1999-2000*	*2000-01*	*2001-02*	*2002-03*	*2003-04*	*2004-05*
Arunachal	13	14	17	17	16	17	17	24
Assam	33	31	31	32	31	29	31	34
Manipur	59	42	36	39	26	28	29	41
Meghalaya	15	17	16	17	18	29	37	45
Mizoram	23	21	24	26	26	26	38	51
Nagaland	18	16	15	14	13	13	17	23
Tripura	34	29	26	23	22	26	25	29
Sikkim	21	20	14	16	16	17	23	30
NER	30	28	27	28	26	26	30	35
All India	56	55	57	59	62	59	59	66

Source: *Dialogue*, Vol. 10, No. 3.

Employment

The employment scenario is rather bad in the north-east compared to other regions of India. There has been a steady downfall of the percentage of cultivators in all the States in the region. This is of course no different from the all-India scenario. The fall has been most significant in the case of Manipur. While there were 59.9 per cent cultivators in 1991 in the State, it came down to 40.2 in 2001. There were barely 27 per cent cultivators in the State of Tripura in 2001. On the other hand, there has been a steady rise in the percentage of agricultural labourers and other workers in almost all the States of the region. This may be interpreted as an indication of gradual pauperization of the region. This is confirmed by the fact that there has been some fall in the percentage of labour force in three of the States—Arunachal Pradesh, Assam and Tripura between 1993-94 and 1999-2000, which is indicated in Table 1.9.

Table 1.9 further confirms the pattern of pauperization. It is found that there has been a sharp fall in the percentage of Main Workers in all the States of North-East between the years 1981 to 2001. On the other hand, there has been a rise in the number of non-workers in the States of Arunachal Pradesh, Assam, Nagaland and Meghalaya during the same period (Table 1.10).

Between 1999-2000 and 2004-05, the problem of unemployment among the youth (15-29 years) of Tripura has worsened manifolds—from 21.4 to 61.4. The political disturbance—ethnic violence could possibly be an important factor for this. Though the rate of literacy is

Table 1.9: Labour Force

States	*1993-94*			*1999-2000*		
	Male	*Female*	*Total*	*Male*	*Female*	*Total*
Arunachal	1.3	0.5	1.0	1.0	0.9	0.9
Assam	4.6	9.5	5.6	3.7	8.0	4.6
Manipur	2.2	1.0	1.8	3.7	3.1	3.5
Meghalaya	0.5	0.3	0.5	0.9	0.9	0.9
Mizoram	0.9	0.5	0.8	2.5	1.3	2.0
Nagaland	3.2	0.6	2.4	4.0	2.9	3.5
Tripura	2.2	8.4	3.4	1.6	4.5	1.9
India	2.1	1.7	2.0	2.5	1.8	2.3

Source: North Eastern Region Vision 2020.

Table 1.10: Changing Composition of Workforce

States	*Main Worker*			*Marginal Worker*			*Non Worker*		
	1981	*1991*	*2001*	*1981*	*1991*	*2001*	*1981*	*1991*	*2001*
Arunachal	49.6	45.2	37.8	3	1	6.2	47.4	53.8	56
Assam	N.A.	31.2	26.7	N.A.	4.9	9.1	N.A.	63.9	64.2
Nagaland	47.5	42.3	35.4	0.7	0.4	7.2	51.8	57.3	57.4
Manipur	40.3	38.6	30.4	2.1	3.6	13.2	56.8	57.8	56.4
Meghalaya	43.4	40.3	32.6	2.5	2.4	9.2	54.1	57.3	58.2
Mizoram	41.7	42.1	40.8	3.7	6.8	11.8	54.6	51.1	47.4
Sikkim	46.6	40.4	39.4	1.7	1.1	9.3	51.7	58.5	51.4
Tripura	29.6	29.1	28.5	2.6	2	7.7	67.7	68.9	63.8
India	33.4	34.1	30.4	3.3	3.4	8.7	63.2	62.5	60.9

Source: North Eastern Region Vision 2020.

quite high in the North-East, that is 71 per cent for Manipur, 63 per cent for Meghalaya, 89 per cent for Mizoram, 67 per cent for Nagaland, 69 per cent for Sikkim, 73 per cent for Tripura, 54 per cent for Arunachal and 63 per cent for Assam while the national average is 65.38 per cent, there is a good number of educated unemployed people in the region. Except for Mizoram the rate of unemployment of all the North-Eastern States are higher than the national average. Even for Mizoram, the data may not reveal the truth as there is a very high percentage of urban population without any sound economic base. In the rural areas too '*jhum* cultivation' has been banned and there is very little practice of settled cultivation (Table 1.11).

Table 1.12 indicates that a very high percentage of the rural population in North-East is involved in the primary sector. Except for Assam, Manipur, Sikkim and Tripura, the persons engaged in the

Table 1.11: Unemployment

States	*Rural*		*Urban*	
	1999-2000	*2004-2005*	*1999-2000*	*2004-2005*
Arunachal	1.5	25.0	11.9	4.9
Assam	12.5	9.7	26.6	2.3
Meghalaya	5.8	3.9	23.1	19.3
Mizoram	3.4	1.3	10.3	4.9
Nagaland	10.0	14.9	28.3	27.7
Sikkim	8.4	7.0	19.0	8.0
Tripura	3.9	33.0	21.4	61.4
India	4.6	5.7	12.4	11.9

Source: North Eastern Region Vision 2020.

Table 1.12: Sectoral Distribution of Workers (2001)

State	*Rural*			*Urban*		
	Primary	*Secondary*	*Tertiary*	*Primary*	*Secondary*	*Tertiary*
Arunachal	83.4	7.5	9.0	8.7	13.4	77.9
Assam	67.7	6.2	26.2	6.0	13.5	80.5
Manipur	75.3	8.9	15.8	28.3	15.6	55.9
Meghalaya	86.5	3.0	10.5	1.3	14.6	84.1
Mizoram	88.5	2.4	12.2	30.3	14.7	55.0
Nagaland	79.7	2.2	18.1	8.4	12.1	79.5
Sikkim	60.8	9.9	29.3	2.1	16.1	81.8
Tripura	45.7	12.0	42.3	2.7	8.0	89.3
India	76.3	11.4	12.4	8.8	32.0	59.2

Source: North Eastern Region Vision 2020.

agricultural sector are significantly more. The secondary sector is not much developed and very few in the area are occupied in this sector. There is a great demand for government service in the urban areas of North-East and not surprisingly a very high percentage are engaged in the tertiary sector. But in States like Manipur and Mizoram, the agriculture and horticultural sector is still in demand and owing to artificial urbanization and conurbation, people from the towns still move out to the adjoining farm lands.

Table 1.13 indicates that the large-scale industries and medium sized industries have a very little presence in the North-East. In States like Assam, Arunachal Pradesh and Nagaland there has been rather a fall in the number of such industries within a gap of five years—1999 to 2003. However, there has been a quantum jump in the case

Table 1.13: The Figures for Large and Medium Industries in NER (As on March 2003)

State	*No. of Units (in 1999)*	*No. of Units (in 2003)*
Arunachal	17	15
Assam	129	120
Manipur	12	12
Meghalaya	10	49
Mizoram	1	1
Nagaland	7	5
Sikkim	N.A.	3
Tripura	2	8
NER	178	213

Source: North Eastern Region Vision 2020.

of Meghalaya. The reasons for this too are unknown. There has been very little expansion in the manufacturing and industrial sector in the North-East, there has been a steady growth rate in the agricultural sector in all the States except Arunachal Pradesh between 1993-94 to 2002-03. It has been considerably higher than the national average which stood at 0.6. The highest has been in the case of Nagaland (12.9).

Fish Production

North-East is a heavy rainfall area and is filled with lot of waterbodies. Most people in the region relish fish as a part of their diet. Fishing is also a popular sport and an important part of the livelihood. Yet there is a large shortfall in the requirements for consumption. Table 1.14 reveals that except for Assam, the per capita fish output is much lower in rest of the States as compared to the national average.

Table 1.14: Fish Production

States	*Total Production (Million Tonnes)*	*Per Capita Output (Kg per head)*
Arunachal	2,650	2.41
Assam	1,80,945	6.79
Meghalaya	6,179	2.68
Mizoram	3,380	3.8
Tripura	17,980	5.62
NER	2,31,847	5.95
India	63,99,390	6.22

Source: North Eastern Region Vision 2020.

Education

The percentage of literacy is quite high in many of the North-Eastern States. Except for Arunachal Pradesh, Assam and Meghalaya the percentage of literacy was higher than the national average (65.38%) in 2001. In Mizoram it was as high as 89 per cent. Though the percentage of literacy has been so good in the region, the rate of dropout from schools between Classes I-X too has been significantly high in North-East. While the national average was 62.6 in 2002-03, it was higher in all the States except Manipur (60.5). The figures in Table 1.15 shows that the rate of dropouts rather went up between 1992-93 and 2002-03 in the States of Meghalaya, Mizoram and Nagaland. Political uncertainty, underground movements and rapid unemployment could be the attributed factors.

Table 1.15: Dropout Rates in Class I to X

States	*1992-93*			*2002-03*		
	Boys	*Girls*	*Total*	*Boys*	*Girls*	*Total*
Arunachal	78.1	80.0	78.8	70.2	73.6	71.7
Assam	74.3	78.1	76.0	74.3	75.7	74.9
Manipur	74.6	75.5	74.5	61.9	59.0	60.5
Meghalaya	67.9	68.1	68.0	81.4	80.5	80.9
Mizoram	57.0	54.4	55.7	77.1	74.1	75.7
Nagaland	75.0	78.2	76.5	77.1	77.9	77.5
Sikkim	85.6	85.7	85.7	76.9	73.1	75.1
Tripura	81.7	83.2	82.4	74.2	74.3	74.3
India	70.0	77.3	72.9	60.7	65.0	62.6

Source: North Eastern Region Vision 2020.

It is evident from Table 1.16 that in North-East India there is a dearth of trained teachers in the schools. All the States in the region have less percentage of trained teachers at the Primary/Upper primary, Middle/Senior Basic and High/Post Basic levels than the national average (86%, 87% and 89% respectively). At the Higher Secondary level except for Meghalaya (98%) all the other States have lower rate of trained teachers than the country as a whole—90 per cent. Though there is a dearth of trained teachers at the school level in the North-East, the pupil/teacher ratio at almost all levels is favourable compared to the national figure. It is only at the Higher Secondary level that in Meghalaya (36) the ratio is slightly more than the national average (35). Not surprisingly, there is a great demand for humanities streams at the higher level of education. It is only in Manipur (35%) that the demand for Science at the higher level is more than the national average (20%).

Table 1.16: Proportion of Trained Teachers and Ratio of Female Teachers

States	*Primary/ Upper Primary*		*Middle/ Senior Basic*		*High/ Post Basic*		*Higher Secondary*	
	Total Trained	*Female*	*Total Trained*	*Female*	*Total Trained*	*Female*	*Total Trained*	*Female*
Arunachal	28	41	33	40	47	32	64	26
Assam	73	53	36	30	30	36	30	40
Manipur	22	63	19	69	28	60	47	80
Meghalaya	45	38	36	85	36	71	98	110
Mizoram	82	94	80	42	64	34	38	79
Nagaland	37	53	42	42	44	59	24	102
Sikkim	50	89	42	56	44	52	51	44
Tripura	28	95	20	36	25	36	34	54
India	86	66	87	69	89	61	90	63

Source: North Eastern Region Vision 2020.

Health

Water borne diseases are quite endemic in many of the North-East States. Not surprisingly the household's access to safe drinking water (Tap, Handpump, Tubewell) was not better than the country as a whole in the States of the region in 2001. The situation was slightly better in the urban areas of only Arunachal Pradesh and Sikkim. There is also acute shortage of drainage system in the region. The situation is slightly better only in the rural areas of Nagaland compared to the entire country. In Nagaland, 61.42 per cent households in rural areas have no drainage as compared to the country (65.82%). However, in the North-East people prefer to use toilets in both rural and urban areas in contrast to other parts of the country. It is only in Arunachal Pradesh and Meghalaya that the situation is otherwise (Table 1.17).

F. Look East Policy (LEP) and the Threat to North-East

Look East Policy was initiated in the year 1991 by the then Prime Minister, Narasimha Rao. The significance and necessity of the LEP

Table 1.17: Household Access to Safe Drinking Water (2001)

States	*Urban*	*Rural*	*Total*
Arunachal	90.7	73.7	77.5
Assam	70.4	56.8	58.8
Manipur	59.4	29.3	37.0
Meghalaya	73.5	29.5	39.0
Mizoram	47.8	23.8	36.0
Nagaland	42.3	47.5	46.5
Sikkim	97.1	67.0	70.7
Tripura	85.8	45.0	52.5
India	90.0	73.2	77.9

Source: North Eastern Region Vision 2020.

was generated by myriads by-product factors of post-Cold War geo-political reconfiguration. It was indeed a foreign policy response of the Government of India to the unfolding global power equation of the post-Cold War era. In spite of initial indications of developing ties with South East Asian nations in the light of regional efforts like the Bandung Conference (1954) and subsequent attempts from Non-Aligned Movement (NAM), India never really made serious efforts to look eastward (Kishan: 2009).

The whole issue of opening the "Eastern Gate" of India pertinently brings in the question of North-East India, whose physical location 'at least' cannot be downplayed if India has to reach out to ASEAN countries, may be in terms of trade and strategic concerns. As the phrase Look East Policy itself suggests, it signifies India's desire for greater competition with and containment of China, and engagement with integration with South-East Asia and ultimately with Asia-Pacific region. The policy is guided by a myriad of interrelated national interests. It is not simply guided by trade as the prime motive but overall politico-economic interest of a burgeoning India *vis-à-vis* emerging geopolitical configuration (Indrakumar: 2009a). At the end of 1980s, India stood out as one of the largest military industry bases in Asia, and commercial prospects for the Indian defence industry in the region looked promising. Besides, India was one of the Asian countries that had a highly developed defence industry and dual use technology that *de facto* made it an important player in the future evolution of the Asian strategic balance (Mezard: 2006).

The entry of Myanmar to the ASEAN Club in 1997 could be an important reason. Since Myanmar is strategically situated betwe[illegible] India and Indo-China, Indian policy-makers may have viewed th[illegible] an alternative way to reach out to East Asia and South-East Asia through Myanmar *via* North-East. Scholars have observed that the Chinese factor is one of the important factors for the shift in India's policies towards East and South-East Asian countries. China is thus seen as "the principal source of insecurity and the greatest potential threat to India's long term interest". Therefore, India's close links with East and South-East Asian countries were considered as possible way to 'set limits on China influence' or perhaps to 'balance' China's expanding power in the region (Gare and Motto: 2003, cited in Barua and Das: 2008). Similarly Renaud (2003) stated three reasons for the strategic interest of Myanmar for India, (i) Instability in the North-East: the Burmese connection, (ii) Reaching out to South-East Asia: the Myanmar Bridge, and (iii) The China Threat.

In view of the previous apathetic attitude of the centre, the current enthusiasm to bring the North-East upfront in India's Look East Policy is certainly an important development. It is because in the past the North-East had never been given importance in India's foreign policy perspectives and even at the time of the announcement of the Look East Policy, the North-East was absolutely inconsequential. In the early literature on the Look East Policy there is no reference to the North-East. Many crucial issues affecting prospects for economic development in the North-East have gone unnoticed in India's foreign policy. For instance, the partition of the country in 1947 blocked the natural sea route through the port city of Chittagong. It landlocked the region and blocked the river transportation route to the sea. This loss of connectivity insulated the economy and affected accessibility to market (Barua and Das: 2008). It is interesting to note that India's threat perception has not changed and the same grand security design continues to inform her Look East Policy. In this projection, there is hardly mentioned any of the possible impact of the policy on the security scenario of the region excepting in very grandiose and general term. The ethnic scenario of the region is thus held captive to India's grand security design (Das: *n.d.*).

The present efforts in connection with LEP to make North-East a "transit point" with no serious attempt to enhance the productive forces of the region for its economic regeneration and development undermine the utility of the policy. The Central Government's ongoing project of constructing a new rail link between Jiriban-Imphal-Moreh (Manipur) at the cost of around INR 2,900 crore and further linking Tamu-Kalay-Sehji at a cost of around INR 1339 crore and

'Cabinet Committee on Economic Affairs' (CCEA) clearance on the proposal to augment the roads networks in the North-East at a cost of INR 12,100 crore, which also includes the connection of the capitals of Nagaland, Meghalaya and Sikkim with the East-West Corridor gives fillip to the above argument (Indrakumar: 2009b). The transnational linkage India plans to draw with the ASEAN countries in the South-East Asia will only ensure partnership role of the NER in the flight paths of capital, even though it may exist as a corridor between India and South-East, while it seeks to join the connected networks of trans-Asian pathways through its capillary geographical contiguity with Myanmar and Bay of Bengal. What waits on this serpentine connectivity is the reduction of NER into a mere node in the already existing sea and land routes surrounded by China (Biswas and Suklabaidya: 2007).

Trade statistics show that India's exports to the East and South-East Asia is dominated by mineral fuels and oil, metallic products, jewellery products, chemicals, iron and steel, ships, boats and floating structures, electrical machinery and equipment, vehicle parts, food and animal fodder and cotton products. Tea, coffee and rubber constitute a very small portion of India's exports to East Asia. During 2005-06, the share of tea, coffee and rubber in India's total exports to East Asia was around 6 per cent. A country-wise analysis shows that India's exports to Indonesia, Malaysia, Thailand, Singapore, China and Myanmar are dominated by manufacturing products. The share of tea, coffee and rubber is negligible. What conclusion could we draw from the above picture? The majority of India's export items consist of manufacturing goods. It is obvious, therefore, that the North-East does not seem to have a comparative advantage in any of India's exports to these countries, given the fact that the share of manufacturing in the domestic product of the region was only 4 per cent in 2003-04 and that manufacturing is growing by a little over 1 per cent. In fact, Assam is the only North Eastern State with some manufacturing orientation, which is non-existent in most other States of the region (Barua and Das: 2008).

The myth created by the Government of India to woo voter of the region that the LEP can be an effective instrument with unlimited scope for the region to engage in international trade with the booming east and the South-East Asian market, which in turn would provide opportunity for industrialization and growth has been rejected by the people of the region. Mere road connectivity with India or the outside world is not a sufficient condition to trigger a development process, as is often believed. The vibrant Indian market is large enough to sustain a process of industrial development in the North-East. It is realized that unless the North-East develops its own regional market, it will not be able to gain much from increased integration. The North-East has potential advantages in many resource-based products which have not yet been properly tapped. However, to develop a comparative advantage in these products, large-scale production and specialization is necessary. Unfortunately, the prevailing transport networks, even within States like Meghalaya, Arunachal Pradesh and Nagaland, are so poor that it has been observed that the production pattern of each State is determined by the self-sufficiency condition rather than production for markets, despite the intrinsic production advantage across States (Barua and Das: 2008). It is clear that the North-East India lacks in many aspects of the infrastructure to generate vibrant economic growth. In fact, the region is handicapped by the absence of industrial and infrastructural base for the competitive market economy, which the policy of India's Look East has brought to its doorstep (Tables 1.18a and 1.18b).

Conclusion

The regional exclusion of North Eastern India can be reflected by the fact that the people other than the North Eastern region called themselves as *mainland India or mainstream India.* The Indian newspaper *Tehelka* in 2006 observed "*for most Indians (North-East India) is on the map but off the mind*". The fact that everything, including the history of North-East India, is neglected by so-called Indian historians (Nag: 1998). History written by India's first Prime Minister, Jawaharlal Nehru, viz., *Glimpse of World History, Discovery of India, Autobiography*, have mentioned Manipur and her people even once (CORE: 2007). North-East India does not get much attention in the English language daily *National Press*. The issues of the region do not make it to the national policy agenda as well (Sonwalkar: 2004; cited in Baruah: 2006). The different development data presented here very clearly indicate the extent of deprivation of the region and this is leading to a feeling of total alienation. End of British colonial domination in the subcontinent in the post-Second World War era did not produce any path breaking changes as the region continued to reel under similar conditions in the face of an

Table 1.18a: India's Import and Export to ASEAN, 2005-06: Top Ten Commodities

Commodity	*Value (US$ million)*	*Share (%)*
Mineral fuels, mineral oils and products of their distillation; bituminous substances; mineral waxes	2,462.94	23.66
Natural or cultured pearls, precious or semi-precious stones, precious metals, clad with precious metal and articles thereof, imitation jewellery, coins	1,590.44	15.28
Organic chemicals	834.34	8.01
Iron and steel	537.28	5.16
Residues and waste from food industries; prepared animal fodder	527.06	5.06
Ships, boats and floating structures	453.33	4.35
Nuclear reactors, boilers, machinery and mechanical appliances; parts thereof	348.58	3.35
Copper and articles thereof	290.54	2.79
Electrical machinery and equipment and parts thereof; sound recorders and reproducers, television image and sound recorders and reproducers, and parts	279.8	2.69
Vehicles other than railway or tramway rolling stock, and parts and accessories thereof	239.94	2.3
Total—top 10 commodities [exports]	**7,564.25**	**72.65**
Total Exports to ASEAN	**10,411.30**	**100,00**

Source: Export-Import Data Bank, Ministry of Commerce, Government of India. [Barua and Das (2008)].

external market, now in the form of the India (other than NER) market and its emergent national capitalist class. The people in North Eastern States referred to it as a neo-colonialism.

Peaceful protests are an outcome of this—as among the Meira Paibis—*The Women Torch Bearer of Manipur*. The Naga Hoho too has been positively taking proactive measure to enhance the peace process. The country on the other hand has undertaken half-hearted measure by some time including the biography of some national heroes of the North-East in the school syllabus. Some cultural troupes are invited to perform in Delhi. Some measures are being undertaken to build people to people contacts. But these are half measures that

Table 1.18b: Top Fifteen Commodities: India's Export to East Asia, 2005-06

Commodity	*Value (US$ million)*	*Share (%)*
Natural or cultured pearls, precious or semi-precious stones, precious metals, clad with precious metal and articles thereof) imitation jewellery, coins.	107.11	10.66
Nuclear reactors, boilers, machinery and mechanical appliances; parts thereof	53.76	5.35
Articles of iron or steel	52.95	5.27
Other made-up textile articles; sets; worn clothing and worn textile articles; rags	52.54	5.23
Articles of apparel and clothing accessories, not knitted or crocheted	46.1	4.59
Iron and steel	45.03	4.48
Articles of leather, saddlery and harness, travel goods, handbags and similar content, articles of animal gut (other than silk worm) gut	35.40	3.52
Pharmaceutical products	34.99	3.48
Mineral fuels, mineral oils and products of their distillation; bituminous substances; mineral waxes	33.49	3.33
Electrical machinery and equipment and parts thereof; sound recorders and reproducers, television image and sound recorders and reproducers, and parts	33.47	3.33
Coffee, tea, mate and spices	30.37	3.02
Organic chemicals	28.70	2.86
Rubber and articles thereof	28.03	2.79
Carpets and other textile floor coverings	26.46	2.63
Miscellaneous chemical products	23.03	2.29
Total—top 15 commodities (exports)	**631.43**	**62.86**
Total Exports	**1,004.50**	**100.00**

Source: Export-Import Data Bank, Ministry of Commerce, Government of India. [Barua and Das (2008)]

have little bearing of the mindset of the people of North-East where the chances of adequate political representation and participation in the national political process is virtually insignificant.

It needs to be reiterated that the exclusion of North-East is a revolt of the very basis of the formation of the Indian nation-state. It is a structural deficiency. Unless the nation-state changes over into a confederation states or nation, there is difficult chance of any improvement. Only portrayal of cultural elements of different North-Eastern communities through exhibitions during the Republic Day Parade or other exhibitions or through the Door Darshan is just a cosmetic effort. The formation of MDONER without any teeth is too just a show.

However, though externally excluded, many of the ethnic entities have strong inclusive cultural elements. The Zikir religious psalms of the native Assamese Muslims resemble the Hindu Assamese Borgits very much. The Pua Mecca of Hajo where there is the temple of Hoygrib Madhav, a Buddhist temple and an Islamic shrine is frequented by people of all faith. The Kamakhya Temple of Guwahati is also considered to be a union of a Khasi mother goddess and the Hindu Shakti goddess Kali. The Roman Catholic Church has incorporated many cultural elements of the native tribes. The agricultural festivals are retained almost in too. The basic structure of the society based on unilinear segmentary system has been barely touched upon. The Meiteis have retained the Tangkhul Naga tribal elements in the annual Lai Haraoba festival. The Nagamese language—a mix of Hindi and Assamese is the common lingua franca of all the Nagas coming from different parts of Nagaland. All the Nagas have accepted the Ao term Nagalim to convey the united nations of the Nagas. It is a gallant sight to find the North-East students studying in different parts of the country congregating to celebrate the regional cultural events together.

REFERENCES

Abercrombie, Nicholas; Hill, Stephen; Turner, Brian (1984), *The Penguin Dictionary of Sociology*, New York.

Ahmed, Rafiul and Prasenjit Biswas (2004), "Political Economy of Under-development of N-E India: Some Conceptual Issues" in Ahmed, Rafiul and Prasenjit Biswas, *Political Economy of Underdevelopment of North-East India*, New Delhi, Akansha Publication.

Akoijam, Bimol and Tarunkumar, Th (2005), "Armed Forces (Special Powers) Act 1958: Disguised War and its Subversions", *Eastern Quarterly*, Volume 3, Issue I, April-June.

Barua, Alokesh and Santosh Kumar Das (2008), "Perspectives on Growth and Development in the North-East: The Look East Policy and Beyond Margin", *The Journal of Applied Economic Research*, 2, 327.

Barua, Alokesh and Bandyopadhyay (2005), "Structural Change, Economic Growth and Regional Disparities in the North-East: Regional and National Perspectives" in Barua (edt.) *India's North-East—Developmental Issues in a Historical Perspective*, New Delhi. Manohar Publication.

Barbora, Sanjoy (2005), "Autonomy in the North East: The Frontiers of Centralized Politics" in Samaddar, Ranabir (edt.), *The Politics of Autonomy—Indian Experiences*, New Delhi. Sage Publication.

Baruah, Sanjib (2005), *Durable Disorder: Understanding the Politics of North East India*, New Delhi, Oxford University Press.

Baruah S. (2006), "Post Frontiers Blues: Towars a New Policy Framework for North East India", *Policy Studies No. 33*, Washington, East West Centre,

Bhobol, S. (2009), Editorial, 'Governance Deviate Peace-Path—Now Ripe for Resolution', *The Orient Vision*, Vol. VI, Issues 1 and 2.

Biswas, Prasenjit and Chandan, Suklabaidya (2007), *Ethnic Life World in North-East India*, New Delhi, Sage Publication.

B.G. Verghese (2008), "Building Northeastern Futures, Looking East", *Eastern Quarterly*; Vol. 4, Issues III and IV, October 2007-March 2008.

Bhaumik, S. (2006). *Ethnicity, Ideology and Religion: Separatist Movements in India's Northeast*, http://www.apcss.org/.ReligiousRadicalism/PagánesfromReligiousRadicalismandSecurityinSouthAsiach10.pdf. (Downloaded on 12th April, 2007).

Brara, N. Vidyalaxmi (2009), "Brushed under the Carpet": Inclusion and Exclusion in Manipur" in Baviskar, B.S. and Mathew George, *Inclusion and Exclusion in Local Governance—Field Studies from Rural India*, New Delhi, Sage Publication.

Chasie, Charles; Hazarika, Sanjay (2009). "The State Strikes Back: India and the Naga Insurgency". *Policy Studies No. 52*. Washington: East West Centre.

Chenoy, Anuradha, M. (2002). *Militarism and Women in South Asia*, New Delhi: Kali for Women,

Corbridge, Stuart, Harris, John, (2000), *Reinventing India: Liberalization, Hindu Nationalism and Popular Democracy*, New Delhi, Oxford University Press.

Das, Samir Kumar (*n.d.*), *Looking East via the Northeast: The Ethnic Dimension*, Calcutta Research Group, Kolkata.

Editorial, *Eastern Quarterly*, Vol. 3, Issue III, October-December 2005.

Edozie, Rita Kiki (2007), "Centralization Trends in Nigeria's PDP Regime:Addressing Pluraslism in Contemporary African Democracies" in Santosh C. Saha, *The Politics of Ethnicity and National Identity*, New York, Peter Lang.

Eller, Jack, David (2002), *From Culture to Ethnicity to Conflict: An Anthropological Perspective on International Ethnic Conflict*, Michigan, The University Press.

Forman, Michael (1956), *Nationalism and the International Labour Movement: The Idea of the Nation in Social and Anarchist Theory*, Pennsylvania, The Pennsylvania State University Press.

Greene, Shane (2008), "Incas, Indios and Indigenism in Peru in Ballve", Teo and Vijay Prashad (edt.) *Dispatches from Latin America: Experiments Against Neoliberalism*, New Delhi. Leftword Books.

Hanjabam, Shukhdeba Sharma (2008), "The Meitei Upsurge in Manipur", *Asia-Europe Journal*, Vol. 6, No. 1.

Hanjabam, Shukhdeba Sharma (2008), "The Youth Panorama in Northeast India", *Asia-Europe Journal*, Vol. 5, No. 4.

Hiral Dave: 31.3.09—*Indian Express*—"Demand for Separate Kutch State picks up pace in poll run-up".

Human Rights Initiatives (2009), "The Deployment of Indian Military Forces in Manipur", *Justice First*, December 08-March 09, Vol. 1, No. 1.

Hussain, Monirul (2008), *Interrogating Development: State, Displacement and Popular Resistance in North East India*, New Delhi, Sage Publication.

Indrakumar, Konthoujam (2009 a), "Mapping India Look East Policy: Shifting Alignments" in Kishan, Thingnam (edt.), *Look East Policy and India's North East: Polemics and Perspectives*, New Delhi, Concept Publishing Company.

Indrakumar, Konthoujam (2009 b), "Imagining the North East Through Look East Policy: Towards a Contextual Understanding", in Kishan, Thingnam (edt.), *Look East Policy and India's North East: Polemics and Perspectives*, New Delhi, Concept Publishing Company.

Jairath, Vinod K. and Srinivas Sajja (2009), "Negotiating with empowerment: Panchayati Raj in Andhra Pradesh" in Baviskar, B.S. and Mathew George, *Inclusion and Exclusion in Local Governance*—Field Studies from Rural India, New Delhi, Sage Publication.

Jensen, Marianne, (2001), Editorial, "Militarization and Human Rights Violations," in *Militarisation, Indigenous Affairs*, Issue 2.

Kishan, Thingnam, (edt.) (2009), *Look East Policy and India's North East: Polemics and Perspectives*, New Delhi, Concept Publishing Company.

Kishan, Thingnam, Singh (2008), *Understanding Underdevelopment: State of Economy in the Northeast*, Vol. 4, Issue III and IV, October 2007-March 2008, pp. 189-200.

Kishwar, Madhu (1999), "Politics of Majoritarianism *vs.* Minoritarianism" Sheth, D.L. and Gurpreet Mahajan (edt.) *Minority Identities and Nation State*, New Delhi, Oxford University Press.

Kotwal, D. (2000), "Instability Parameters in Northeastern India". *Strategy Anal* XXIV(1):137–149.

Kunal Chattopadhyay, Aninda Bannerjee, Saurobbijoy Sarkar (2005), *The Permanent Revolution and Results and Prospects—Leon Trotsky*, New Delhi, Aakar Books.

Lalrintluanga (2009), "Mizoram: Development of Politico-Administrative System and Statehood", New Delhi: Serial Publications.

Louis, Prakash (n.d.), *Social Exclusion: A Conceptual and Theoretical Framework*, http://www.empowerpoor.org/downloads/Social_Exclusion_PACS_final.pdf, downloaded on April 9, 2009.

Nag, S. (1998), *India and Northeast India—Mind Politics and the Process of Integration*. Delhi, Regency Publication,

Nunthara, C. (1981), "Grouping of Village in Mizoram: Its Social and Economic Impact," *Economic and Political Weekly*, Special Article, July 25.

Madhab, Jayanta (1999), North-East: Crisis of Identity, Security and Underdevelopment, *Economic and Political Weekly*, February, 6.

Mezard, Isabelle Saint (2006), *East ward Bound—India's New Positioning in Asia*, New Delhi, Manohar Publication.

Ministry of Development for North Eastern Region (M-DONER) and North Eastern Council (NEC) (2008), *North Eastern Region: Vision 2020*.

Mukhim, Patricia (2006), "Negotiating Ethnic Identity in a Democracy" in B.B. Kumar, *Problems of Ethnicity in the North-East India*, New Delhi, Concept Publishing Company.

Nongbri, T. (2001), "Timber Ban in North-East India: Effects on Livelihood and Gender", *EPW*, May 26.

Peace, "Progress and Prosperity" in the Northeastern *Region: Vision 2020*, Vol. I, 2007.

Parratt, John (2005), *Wounded Land: Politics and Identity in Modern Manipur*, New Delhi, Mittal Publication.

Priyoranjan. Ch. Singh, "Manipur Economy: Historical Roots and Structural Evolution," *Eastern Quaterly*, Vol. 3, Issue III, October-December 2005, pp. 149-159.

Ramananda, "Wagkheirakpam and Yumnam, Jiten, Insidious Financial Intrusions in India's North East," New Delhi: *Intercultural Resources and Forum for Indigenous Perspectives and Action, 2006*.

Rangasami, Amrita, (1978), "Mizoram—Tragedy of our Own Making," *Economic and Political Weekly*, April 17.

Renaud, Egreteau (2003), "India and Burma/Myanmar Relations: From Idealism to Realism," *Conference Paper*.

Robinson, Andrew (2005), *The Rhizomes of Manipur*, Seminar Paper, Institute of Asia Pacific Studies, University of Nottingham.

Rodgers, Gerry, Charles G. Gore, Jose B. Figueiredo (1995), *Social Exclusion: Rhetoric, Reality, Responses* (International Institute for Labour Studies, United Nations Development Programme).

Roy Burman, B.K. (*n.d.*), *The Other Manipur, Politics in the North-East*, Kanglaonline.com

Roy Burman, B.K. (2000), "Social Factors of Development in Manipur", in M. Horam (edt.), *The Rising Manipur including other North Eastern States*, New Delhi, Manas Publications.

Roy Burman, J.J. (1999), "Pluralism and Nationalism: Some Reference to Northeast India," *Journal of the Indian Anthropological Society*, Volume 34, No. 3, November.

Roy Burman, J.J. (2001), "Manipur: Of Accords and Discords," *One Indian One People*, September.

Rudolph, Lloyd I. and Susanne Hoeber Rudolph, (2008), "Explaining Indian Democracy: A Fifty-Year Perspective, 1956-2006," Vol. III. *The Realm of the Public Sphere: Identity and Policy*. New Delhi, Oxford University Press.

Sanajaoba, Naorem (2006), *Armed Forces Special Power Act*, 1958—*A Law for Extrajudicial Execution in Perpetuity*, Paper at AASU-Apunba Lup, one day convention, Guwahati.

Sengupta, Dipankar (2005), "Unwriting Accomplices: State as Agents of Inequality" in Barua (edt.) *India's North-East—Developmental Issues in a Historical Perspectives*, New Delhi, Manohar Publication.

Sheth, D.L. (1999), "*The Nation State and Minority Rights*" in Sheth, D.L. and Gurpreet Mahajan (edt.) *Minority Identities and Nation State*, New Delhi, Oxford University Press.

Shils, Edward (1975), *Centre and Periphery: Essays in Macrosociology*. Chicago: University of Chicago Press.

Singh, R.R. (2003), "Reducing social exclusion through social intervention" in A.K. Lal, *Social Exclusion: Essays in Honour of Dr. Bindeshwar Pathak*, New Delhi, Concept Publishing Company.

Centre for Organization Research and Education (2002), "Manipur: A Report on Impunity of Human Rights Violations under the Armed Forces (Special Powers) Act, 1958, Amended 1972." Submitted to the *Special Rapporteur on the Human Rights and Fundamental Freedoms of Indigenous People*.

Sonowal, C.J. (2008), "Indian Tribes and Issue of Social Inclusion and Exclusion," *Study of Tribes and Tribals*, 6(2): 123-134.

Subramanian, K.S. (2007), *Political Violence and the Police in India*, New Delhi, Sage Publication.

Thakkar, Himanshu (2005), "*Big Dams in Northeast India*—For whose benefits? For What benefits?" In Menon, Manju and Kanchi Kohli (comp), *Large Dams for Hydropower in Northeast India*. New Delhi, *Kalpavarish and South Asia Network on Dams, Rivers and People*.

United Committee Manipur, (2005), *Influx of Migrants into Manipur: A Threat to the Indigenous Ethnic People*, Imphal.

Vagholikar, Neeraj, (2007), *A Flood of Dams*, Himalmag, http://www.himalmag.com/2007/september/arunachal_pradesh_hydropower.htm

Ward, David and Elisabeth, Farmaki (2006), *Loosening the Social Exclusion Knot and Exploring the Chemistry of Social Inclusion*, Working Paper Series, Social Science Research Network.

Yumnam, Amar (2005), *Development Intervention in Northeast: A Critique*, Vol. 3, Issue III, October-December 2005, pp. 196-2005.

2
Roots of Self-Determination Movements in India's North-East

Shukhdeba S. Hanjabam

Introduction

Primarily the concern for right to self-determination is embedded in the issue of human rights. Human rights are rights held by individuals simply because they are part of the human species. They are rights shared equally by everyone regardless of sex, race, nationality, and economic background. They are universal in content. Across the centuries, conflicting political traditions have elaborated different components of human rights or differed over which elements had priority. The manifold meanings of human rights reflect the process of historical continuity and change that helped their present substance and helped form the Universal Declaration of Human Rights adopted by the General Assembly of the United Nations in 1948 (Ishay: 2004).

The right to self-determination, a fundamental principal of human rights law, is an individual and collective right to "freely determine... political status and [to] freely pursue... economic, social and cultural development". The International Court of Justice (ICJ) refers to the right to self-determination as a right held by people rather than a right held by governments alone (Parker: 2000). The right to self-determination is a right which reflects the importance given to communities, collectives and families in many societies and the general inherent communal quality of humans. The purpose of the protection of this right is to enable these communities as communities to prosper and transmit their culture as well as participate fully in the political, economic and social processes, thus allowing the distinct character of a community "to have this character reflected in the institutions of government under which it lives". It also forms part of the empowering process of human rights. Thus, the right protects people from being subject to oppression by subjugation, domination or exploitation because, as the African Charter makes clear, "nothing shall justify the domination of a people by another" (McCorquodale: 1994). It is also seen as a right of dominated peoples to achieve equality in relation to those who dominate them.

An important and influential factor with respect to the emergence and historical development of the concept of self-determination is formed by the phenomenon of communities refusing to consent, or accept any longer, the exercise of power over them by the ruler or government of group consciousness and political awareness, these communities repudiated the rights of an elite or an "alien" people to determine for them and without their consultation their fate, their destiny, and their political, cultural, social and economical status. It is this claim of people to govern themselves which find expression in both the American and French Revolutions. These revolutions were based on natural law theory insofar as they reflected a rejection of the Divine Rights of Kings (Raic: 2002).

John Locke had asserted as early as 1667 that the people were supreme and that government was fiduciary. In his *Treatise Essay Concerning Toleration,* he declared that the authority of Magistrates was to be exercised only for the 'good, preservation and peace of men in that society' and that their conduct must in consequence be governed by this standard alone. The importance of civil liberty, natural rights, and popular sovereignty was also emphasized by other English political philosophers of this period, including James Harrington, Algernon Sidney, and John Milton, in *The Tenure of Kings and Magistrates*, noted that the 'power of Kings and Magistrates is nothing else, but what is only derivatives, transferred and committed to them in trust from the people, to the common good of them all, in whom the power yet remains fundamentally, and cannot be taken from them without a violation of their natural birthright. Harrington in his work *Oceana,* sought to envisage a model commonwealth. He emphasized that civil liberty would be absolutely fundamental to such a commonwealth, and that its laws would derive from reason, and receive the consent of all. Liberty and equality would be guaranteed by the fundamental law or constitution (Musgrave: 1997).

In the eighteenth and nineteenth centuries, right to self-determination was evolved simultaneously in Europe and the United States. In Western Europe and the United States the notion of self-determination drew its inspiration primarily from Enlightenment ideas of popular sovereignty and representative government. Self-determination in the Western Europe context was democratic, ongoing, and universal in character. In Central and Eastern Europe, on the other hand, the notion of self-determination was based primarily on the nineteenth century phenomenon of nationalism. This means that in Western Europe and the United States, the concept had a political orientation which generally did not take ethnic considerations into accounts, whereas in Central and Eastern Europe the concept was much more strongly linked to ethnic and cultural factors (*ibid.*).

Although the debate about the definition and application of self-determination originated and evolved with the disintegration of empires within and beyond Europe, it resurfaced whenever a group sought full participation in the community of states. During the World War-I and in its immediate aftermath, both V.I. Lenin and U.S. President, Woodrow Wilson advocated the adoption of self-determination of peoples as a principle to guide international relations. Lenin promoted its application to ethnic or national groups; colonial peoples; and populations subject to territorial redistribution. He argued that all ethnic groups, not only those under colonial domination, should be able to freely determine their own fate, either through secession or autonomy within a federation, even through force of arms. Similarly, Wilson vowed that peoples should not be "bartered about ... as though they were mere chattels and pawns in a game". However, for the US President self-determination was the right of all peoples to choose their form of government, through peaceful, democratic means and not armed struggle. Wilson's draft article on self-determination was not inserted into the final text of the Covenant. This result reflected the significant resistance by the victorious powers to the universal application of self-determination. By way of a concession, those groups whose exercise of self-determination was thwarted were provided with other, more limited political, social and cultural rights in the form of minority guarantees (Ana: 2008).

The universal human right—the right to self-determination and independence is within the framework of the United Nations Charter.

By a joint reading of Article 2(4), Article 1(2) and Article 55 of the United Nations Charter, the principles are quite clear for practice in that the dependent peoples have the inalienable right to self-determination and no member of the U.N. has the prerogative to use any force or even threat not to speak of force against such peoples, who struggle for freedom and independence. However, the use of force by the colonized people or dominated people cannot be equated with the use of force by aggressor (Sanjaoba: 1995). The momentous and historic Declaration on the Granting of Independence to Colonial Countries and Peoples, adopted by the General Assembly on 14 December, 1960 in its resolution 1514 (XV) which has been termed the Magna Carta of decolonization and which marks the beginning of the modern attitude to the subject and of the irreversible trend towards full decolonization (Espiell: 1980). It is followed closely by the International Covenant on Civil and Political Rights and International Covenant on Economic, Social and Cultural Rights of 1966. It was in accordance with the wishes of the assembly was expressed in 1952 that both the ICCPR and the ICESCR included the right of self-determination in their Common Article 1 (Cop & Dogan: 2005). The Declaration on Principles of International Law Concerning Friendly Relation and Co-option among States in Accordance with the Charter of the United Nations 1970 was adopted by the General Assembly on 25th anniversary of the UN Charter and the Declaration on the Rights of Indigenous Peoples adopted by the General Assembly Resolution 61/295 on 13th September, 2007.

The struggle of the dependent or, dominated or, colonized peoples against racist or, alien or, colonial rule in the exercise of their right to self-determination had been recurrently approved along with the above-mentioned declaration, by the following General Assembly Resolutions: 2599 B (XXIV) of 15th December, 1969; 2649 (XXV) of 30th November, 1970; 2787 (XXVI) of 6th December, 1971; 2955 (XXVII) of 12th December, 1972; 3070 (XXVIII) of 30th November, 1973; 3246 (XXIX) of 29th November, 1974); 3382 (XXX) of 10th November, 1975 (Sanajaoba:1995).

India has signed and ratified the International Covenant on Civil and Political Rights and International Covenant on Economic, Social and Cultural Rights of 1966 in 10th April, 1979 with a reservation on Article 1 of the two covenants which talk about the right of self-determination of the people. The Indian representative to the U.N. addressed the General Assembly on 20th November, 1991 urging upon the world body to work earnestly to eradicate the remaining vestiges of colonialism before entering the twenty first century. He pleaded for the decolonization of Western Sahara, New Caledonia and the Malvinas, among others (Sanajaoba: 1995). As the historical records speak, India had been consistently supporting the militant struggles of ANC, Vietnam, PLO, Bangladesh Mukti Bahini and nearly every decolonization movement in the world irrespective of the methods the Non-State Entities resort to. In East Pakistan, India sent all her troops to liberate the Bengalis subjugated by their lawful government (Sanajaoba: 2002). In January 1949, Nehru conveyed an altogether different conference in New Delhi which was exclusively devoted to the plight of Indonesia. Several Asian countries and Australia participated in the conference. Resolutions were passed which asked the Dutch to release the Indonesian leaders and to grant independence to Indonesia by 1950 (Rothermund: 2006). But unfortunately, the legitimate aspirations of the self-determination movements in their own continent are concealed from decolonization process.

In the North-East India, the resistance groups, regional parties and youth unions, among others, had of late been claiming their right to self-determination in varying degrees and modalities on the grounds that for historical reasons, the North Eastern States, remained outside the Indian fold till the signing of the Yandaboo Treaty and that Assam had been economically, culturally and politically colonized by the Indian Government. Manipur had enunciated on the ground by adopting armed struggle since 1948-49, its claim to exercise the Right to self-determination by stipulating the reasons that save during historical cataclysms and consequently after the disputed merger with India in 1949, it remained an independent country for two and half millennia. The self-determination movements in the entire North-East of India which was sparked off by communist armed struggle in 1948-49 in Manipur and the subsequent Naga upsurge in 1950s, Mizo and Tripura in the 60s and had touched upon Assam in the late 1980s. Although Manipur scene share commonality with the other self-determination movements elsewhere in the world and the North Eastern States in her proximity, Manipuri's claim to exercise her Right to self-determination is clearly demonstrated by a host of politico-historical and legal justification that might not be conveniently refuted nor contradicted lest an impartial international tribunal should decide the issue. Unlike Kashmir it is least known (Sanajaoba *op.cit*).

The right to self-determination is indisputably a norm of "*jus cogens*". *Jus cogens* norms are the highest rules of international law and they must be strictly obeyed at all times. Both the international Court of Justice and the Inter-America Commission on Human Rights of Organisation of American States have ruled on cases in a way that supports the view that the principal of self determination also has the legal status of '*erga omnes*'. The term "*erga omnes*" means "flowing to all". According, *ergas omnes* obligations of a State are owed to the international community as a whole: when a principle achieves the status of *erga omnes* the rest of the international community is under a mandatory duty to respect it in all circumstances in their relations with each other (Parker: 2000). Similarly, Halim Moris observe that, the right to self-determination is considered *jus cogens*, and a part of customary international law that imposes binding obligations on all nation-states. It is considered not simply a principle of international law, but rather an affirmative right of *all peoples*. It is seen as a prerequisite to any genuine enjoyment of any of the human rights. But despite notable recognition of the right to self-determination, there is still a great deal of disagreement among states, and among international scholars, as to the scope and parameters of the right to self-determination, as well as *who*, exactly, is entitled to such a right (Halim Moris, no date).

The two important United Nations studies on the right to self-determination set out factors of a people that gives rise to possession of right to self-determination: a history of independence or self rule in an identifiable territory, a distinct culture, and a will and capacity to retain self-governance (Parker *op. cit.*).

Self-Determination Movements in India's North-East

The self-determination movement in India's North-East is a part of the larger movement against the colonial forces in the world particularly in South Asia and South-East Asian countries. In the late nineteenth and early tweentieth century, movements demanding right to self-determination were organized in European, Asian and American colonies. The Indian National Congress (1885), The Zionist Movement (1896), and movements of Sinn Fein in Ireland (1905), The All India Muslim League (1906), and the Arab Congress (1913) were among the first. They were later joined after the World War-I, by non-communist anti-Colonial movements in Korea (1919), China

(1922), and Indonesia (1927), and by Communist parties in Korea (1919), and Indo-China (1925). Initially, these movements demanded for a greater say in the colonial government but later turned out to demand for full sovereignty or freedom like 'Home Rule' in Ireland, '*Swaraj*' in India, 'doc lap' in Indo-China. This ignited the ideas of exercising right to self-determination to create their own states (Schaeffer: 1999).

The self-determination movements were witnessed in the State of Manipur in the late 40s, Nagaland in the 40s, Mizoram and Tripura in the 60s and Assam in the late 70s. Meghalaya and Arunachal are more of resting place for the bigger resistance groups. The demand by the resistance group can be broadly divided between independence or secession and autonomy or anything beyond Independence. Binalakshmi Nepram observed that the region has become the "South Asia Fractured Frontier". The intention of this chapter is to cover only the root causes of the armed self-determination movement. So it is limited mainly to the initial phase of the movement. This chapter begins with Manipur and is followed by States of Nagaland, Mizoram, Assam and Tripura. Arunachal and Meghalaya are not considered in this chapter (Table 2.1).

Manipur

Manipur had established a sophisticated kingdom at a time when State formation was unknown to most parts of the region. As per the Manipur State Archives, she was ruled by 76 kings since 33 A.D. The Kingdom was governed based on the written constitution "*Loiyumba Shinyen*". This decree was issued by King Loiyumba in 1110 A.D. and was based on the earlier codes and conventions. Manipur was recognized by foreign nations, especially by the Shan with the *1470 Agreement between the King Kiyamba of Manipur and Khekhomba of Pong* in upper Burma. It was followed by the *Anglo-Manipur Friendship Treaty in 1762, Anglo-Manipuri Defence Protocol of 1763, Treaty of Yandaboo, 1826* after the Burmese occupied Manipur (1819-1826—remembered as "Seven Year Devastation") (Hanjabam: 2008). Not only have the Meiteis possessed a distinct political and territorial status for centuries, they also have a highly literate and developed culture, an advanced literary tradition which stretches back a thousand years, and a distinctive linguistic tradition (Chandhoke: 2006).

Table 2.1: Tracing the Origin of the Armed Struggle in India's North-East

Sl. No.	*Year*	*Happenings*
1.	1940s	Struggle for independence starts in Nagaland and Manipur. Struggle was by peaceful means.
2.	Early 1960s	Groups of militants (Naga and Manipuris) go to China *via* Kachin Corridor for arms and training. China provides these free of cost.
3.	Late 1960s	Militants return with Chinese arms and ammunitions. Help also comes from Pakistan. Mizo insurgency starts off after the 'Mautam' famine episode.
4.	1970s	■ Training of insurgents and supplies taken over by Burmese rebels... for a price. ■ Militancy in Assam starts in protest against illegal migration.
5.	1980s	■ A prairie fire of militancy engulfs the three States of Manipur, Nagaland and Mizoram. ■ Drug addiction on the rise in the North-East. ■ Boom time of opium cultivation in Myanmar and other Golden Triangle Areas.
6.	1990s	■ First HIV case detected. HIV/AIDS epidemic spreads in the region due to intravenous drug using. ■ Ethnic clashes start occurring between: Kuki-Naga (Manipur) Kuki Paite (Manipur) Tribals-Non-Tribals (Tripura) Reangs *vs.* Mizo (Mizoram) Boro *vs.* Santhals (Assam) Assamese *vs.* Illegal Migrants (Assam)
		■ Insurgency engulfs the comparatively peaceful States of Meghalaya, Tripura and Arunachal Pradesh. Mayhem unleashed in Tripura.

Source: Mentschel, Binalakshmi (2007).

The British administered Manipur directly from 1891-1907 after she was defeated in 1891 in Anglo-Manipur War. The annexation of Manipur by the British was debated in the British Parliament for illegally occupying an independent Kingdom and thus Manipur was not annexed and allowed to remain as a princely state followed by limited monarchy till 1947. Thus, the status of the former sovereign state had been reduced to that of a Princely State with 11 gun salute. On 15th August, 1947, the British left Manipur. Accordingly, she regained her independence after 56 years. The King surrendered power to the people in order to form a democratic government. The Maharaja appointed both the dominant Meitei leaders and representatives of the Naga and Kuki groups as member of the Drafting Committee of Manipur State Constitution in 1947. The Constitution of the Constituent Assembly was announced by the Maharaja on 10-03-1947. The members were (1) F.F. Pearson (PSMD), Chairperson; (2) S. Somerendro Singh; (3) Md. Kazi Walliullah (representing the Darbar); (4) L.M. Ibungohal Singh (chief court); (5) S. Bijoy Singh (Jiribam); (6) A. Ibotombi Singh (non-official); (7) H. Dwijamani Dev Sharma; (8) Dr. L. Leiren Singh; (9) L. Jogeshwari Singh; (10) S. Krishnamohan Singh; (11) Mera Jatra (five representatives from the Valley); (12) Daiho; (13) Thangkhopao; (14) Tiangkham; (15) Teba Kilong; and (16) R. Suisa (five representatives from the Hills) (Maipaksana: 1995). During the discussion, secession of the hills after five years was proposed by Daiho—a Mao Naga but it was rejected by the Committee. Later, a Kabui Naga person too was also included as a member into the Drafting Committee.

The Manipur Constitution Act 1947 included 53 members of Legislative Assembly, in that 18 seats were reserved for the hills but not on the basis of tribes, the remaining seats were for the valley including Mohammedans. Every community was represented except the Mao as there was no election due to political agitation. After the election, a fully responsible government was formed for the first time in the history of Manipur. The election of 1948 was the endorsement of the State by the people of Manipur in a democratic way. There were 8 Naga MLAs, i.e., 5 Tangkhuls, 2 Zeliangrongs and one Monshang; the other 9 were Kuki-Chins including Kom and Paite. The representatives of the hill tribes were appointed as Ministers of the State which had never occurred in the history of Manipur. The hill people accepted the Maharaja as the symbol of unity of the kingdom. This symbol was destroyed when the State was merged with the Dominion of India in October 1949. The relation between Manipur and the Dominion of India was guided by the Instrument of Accession and the Stand Still Agreement signed by Maharaja of Manipur. Manipur was an autonomous State with complete internal independence though she accepted Indian currency, post and telegraph, foreign affairs and defence (Kamei: 2003). The clauses 7 and 8 of the Instrument of Accession clearly stated the sovereignty status of Manipur. It reads,

> Clause 7, "Nothing in this Instrument shall be deemed to commit me in any way to acceptance of any future Constitution of India or to fetter my discretion to enter into arrangements with Government of India under any such future condition".

> Clause 8, "Nothing in this Instrument affects the continuance of my sovereignty in and over this State, or save as provided by or under this Instrument, the exercise of any powers, authority and rights now enjoyed by me a Ruler of this State".

Table 2.2: Transformation of Manipur State

Sl. No.	*Period*	*Status of State*	*Order*
1.	Pre 1947*	International Protectorate	1
2.	26th July, 1947	Autonomous State (Constitution Adopted)	2
3.	11th August 1947	Associate State (Sovereign within Indian Confederation)	3
4.	15th August 1947	Sovereign State	4
5.	18th October, 1948	Sovereign Peoples Republic (Assembly Function)	5
6.	15th October, 1949	Annexed State (Continuous State with suspended sovereignty)	6
7.	21st January, 1972	Constituent State of India (Suspended Sovereignty)	7

* Political status of states during the inter-war period (1919-1945) had varied in the comity of nations.

Categories altered.

Source: Sanajaoba (1995b).

The dominion of India was fully aware of the political development in Manipur from the very beginning after British departure. Mr. Akbar Hydari, Governor of Assam was involved in the development of the Manipur State Interim Council, 1947. He advised that the Council should comprise Mr. F.F. Pearson as Chief Minister, three official Manipuri members of which one should be the Muslim member of the then existing State Council (established in 1-7-47), two members should be elected on the same franchise and one Hillman be nominated to form a member of that Committee (Singh, M.: 1993). But when the King insisted that he was powerless to sign the merger as he is only a constitutional head. (He added that the power lies with the Manipur Legislative Assembly.) He found himself to be a prisoner in the hands of Sri Prakasa—Governor of Assam. His house was encircled by armed security personnel. The Maharaja was absolutely cut off from the outside world. The Government of India in order to ink the agreement, stated that, the dominion of India throughout, dealt with Maharaja directly as a Ruler of the State, and they were not prepared to make any deviation from the procedure then followed (Singh, K.: 1989).

Except for a few, people of Manipur by and large were opposed to the merger with India. The Praja Santi Sabha, the ruling party of that time expressed from the very beginning that Manipur remain as a state enjoying responsible government with His Highness, the Maharaja of Manipur as the Constitutional Head and with her sovereignty undisturbed. The Manipur State Congress was demanding the merger of Manipur but in their election manifesto of 1948, there was complete silence of pro-merger statements. The general public through a meeting at Gandhi Maidan on 3rd August, 1949, under the joint presidentship of Solet Haokip Kuki, Habi Dewan Mohammed and Nandalal Sharma resolved against the proposed integration or merger of Manipur particularly against the decision of the Manipur Congress Party. The Manipur daily *Bhagyabati Patrica* tried to mould public opinion against the merger (*op. cit.*). Similarly, the Manipur Students' Federation held a protest rally by hosting a Black Flag at Porompat (presently under Imphal east district) on 15 August, 1949. All the members of political parties besides the Congress in the Legislative Assembly adopted resolution against the merger (Nag: 2002). The legendary leader Irabot has already mobilized people for an independent Manipur.

The Sovereignty of Manipur was short-lived as Manipur merged with India amidst allegations that Maharaja signed the merger '*under coercion*' on 21st September, 1949. The circumstances under which Manipur merged into India completely bypassing the elected representatives still remains contentious (Chandhoke: 2006). When Mr. Prakasa—Governor of Assam informed Sardar Vallabhbhai Patel that the King is reluctant to sign the merger without the consent of the State Assembly and the people of Manipur. He responded to use force by sending a telegram "Isn't there a brigadier in Shillong?" to instrument the merger. The reasons cited for the decision to '*take over*' Manipur are revealing: Manipur is a '*border state*' and '*backward*' and, therefore, a '*strategic necessity*'! Curiously, the phrase used by V.P. Menon, the 'arch manoeuvrer' of the integration policy, is not '*integrate*' or '*integration*' but '*take over*' of Manipur (Akoijam and Tarunkumar: 2005). Sanajaoba observed that under this condition, there will be no country that will not be annexed by USA because one country is a border to another country (Sanajaoba: 1995).When the ceremony which proclaimed an end to the ancient kingdom took place on 15th October, 1949 in Imphal, the Indian army was in place to guard against possible trouble (Baruah: 2006).

Irabot went underground on 21st September, 1948 during the protest meeting against the proposed 'Purvanchal Scheme' at Manipur Dramatic Union Hall. While remaining underground he succeeded in engaging the peasants as well as the Communist Party. His weekly *Anouba Jug* appeared regularly with no interruption. Above all, he managed to distribute many leaflets, pamphlets and also issued political statements from time to time. Because of the people's support, the government was unsuccessful in arresting Irabot. In March 1950, "Red Guard" was formed as an armed group. The Red Guard had its camp at Kangmong, North Jiri, Bandiya (Near Nambol), etc. In order to intensify the armed movement, Irabot went to Burma to seek help. The three factions of Communist Party in Burma was reconciled and formed a 'Unified Front Liberation Government of Burma' (UFLGB) with the effort of Irabot by organizing a tripartite conference of the three parties. In recognizing his contribution, an agreement was reached that UFLGB will give the Kabaw Valley and Ango-Ching to Manipur. This area became a general headquarters of Irabot. Unfortunately, Irabot died without realizing his dream of an "Independent Socialist Republic of Manipur" in South East Asia at his headquarters Kabaw Valley on 26th September, 1951 (Rajendra: 2006). When Irabot died, the underground movement could not last long as his overground comrades had given up the fight and were involved in the State politics.

The Red Guard's revolution in 1950-51 left a profound, indelible impact on the informed Manipuri worldview and onward progression of a composite, egalitarian history of the ancient Asian state (Sanajaoba: 2008). Manipur Revolutionary Nationalist Party

(MRNP) was formed in 1953 to complete the task of Red Guard but it was short-lived. The Meitei State Committee in the late 1950s was faded before they could make any significant development. The movement was followed by different groups since today with some of the groups in a very systematic and sustained character. The United National Liberation Front (UNLF) was formed in 1964 under the leadership of (i) President: Kalalung Kamei of Tameglong, (ii) Vice-President: Khangsopao Singshit of Karong, and (iii) General Secretary: Arambam Somorendra of Imphal. In 1968, a breakaway political group established a government-in-exile called the Revolutionary Government of Manipur (RGM) with headquarters at Sylhet in erstwhile East Pakistan (now Bangladesh), with the objective of 'Liberating Manipur through armed struggle'. In September 1978, the People's Liberation Army (PLA), with a Leftist ideology and alleged training in guerrilla warfare in China, was founded by N. Bisheswar an educated Meitei youth. The Revolutionary People's Front (RPF) and its military wing, the People's Liberation Army (PLA) have signed the Common Article 3rd of the Fourth Geneva Convention in 1997 and also have submitted a memorandum to the UN Decolonization Committee (Committee of 24; Sanajaoba: 2006). Subsequently, Manipur also witnessed the growth of a number of other militant underground organizations since 1970s (Table 2.3).

Many organizations have faded away breaking into many factions. It is mainly because of the loss of cadres or their leaders killed or arrested. Extortion, kidnapping, threatening, looting are the order of the day for some of these organizations. They are no more a resistance group whom the people use to support. The government also created armed group to counter the original resistance groups. In order to protect their own communities, each and every community has developed its own armed group. Most of them have emerged after the infamous Kuki-Naga conflict in the early 1990s. Some of the powerful groups like the KNA/KNO claimed to form the Kuki Land or Kuki Homeland by merging some hill districts of Manipur. Similar is the case of Greater Nagaland. It contradicts the claim of the resistance groups fighting for Independent Manipur. This has created a conflict between the UNLF and KNO/KNA some years back. But the Kuki-Chin-Mizo group (19 groups) which was earlier fighting with demand ranging from Autonomy/Union territory is negotiating with the State Government. But it is to be noted that the boundary of Manipur will not be disturbed by the ongoing talk. The

Table 2.3: Strength of Active Outfits in Manipur

Outfits	*Approximate Cadre Strength*	*Weapons and Explosives*	*Area of Influence*
UNLF	2,250-2,500	A.K series rifles, M-16 rifles, UMG, mortars, pistols, grenade launchers, Chinese grenade.	Valley districts and some parts of hill districts
PLA	1,200-1,500	A.K series rifles, M-16 rifles, UMG, mortars, pistols, grenade launchers, IEDs, Chinese grenade.	Valley Districts
KYKL	500-600	A.K series rifles, M-16 rifles, SLRs, Sniper rifles, pistols, grenade launchers.	Valley Districts
PREPAK	400-500	A.K series rifles, M-16 rifles, SLRs, Sniper rifles, pistols, grenade launchers.	Valley districts
PULF	75-90	A.K series rifles, pistols.	Thoubal, Imphal-East and Imphal-West
KCP	100	A.K series rifles, pistols.	Imphal-East, Imphal-West and Bishnupur
NSCN-IM	6000	A.K series rifles, M-16 rifles, UMG, mortars, pistols, grenade launchers, IEDs, Chinese grenade.	Hill districts
NSCN-K	600-750	A.K series rifles, pistols, IEDs, Chinese grenade.	Hill districts

Source: Routray (2009).

factional fight between the UNLF and KYKL that have created a fear in Manipur is now working together. UNLF, PLA, PREPAK have started to work together under a common platform "Manipur People's Liberation Front" since 1st March, 1999. The UNLF with support from PLA and PREPAK have fought back the army offensives in 2005 in order to continue holding part of Manipur as a 'Liberated zone' (Table 2.4).

Table 2.4: Roadmap to Peace in Manipur

Sl. No.	*Year*	*Actor*	*Demand*	*Result*
1.	February 28, 2001	Manipur Government	Ceasefire	Failed
2.	November 26, 2000	UNLF	Sovereignty of Manipur	No response from Government
3.	January 31, 2005	UNLF	Sovereignty of Manipur through Plebiscite	No response from Government
4.	2008	PLA	Talk only on Issue of independence and sovereignty of Manipur	No response from Government

Source: Compiled by Author.

In order to tackle the situation, Manipur was declared a disturbed area and the Armed Forces Special Powers Act (AFSPA) 1958 was imposed in September 1980 which legitimised full-scale military operations, permitting even a non-commissioned officer to kill anyone on mere suspicion with guaranteed immunity. Later, a series of successful counter-insurgency operations resulted in the effective decimation of the major groups. The militancy, however, re-emerged in force towards the end of the 1980s. In the period of 1980–May 30, 2007, 2,675 civilians, 1,314 militants were killed, 2,061 civilians were injured and only 865 surrendered to the government authorities (POKNAPHAM, 16th July, 2007). In 2008 with 497 deaths recorded surpassing the 408 deaths in 2007. The fatalities figure put Manipur in the top of the armed violence in India after Jammu and Kashmir. According to unofficial sources, at least 20,000 people may have died due to violence since the conflict began in the 1950s. But Manipur, a small State of two million people, is tucked away in the country's remote north-eastern region. Not much that happens there makes the national news—unless it is a particularly brutal attack by militants (*Human Rights Watch*: 2008).

The dominant resistance groups of Manipur particularly the PLA and UNLF have not expressed their desire to talk with the government since inception. On November 26, 2000, the UNLF, Chairperson, R.K. Meghen, put forward three conditions for talks with the Centre:

1. The Centre should include the agenda of sovereignty if it was truly serious about its offer of talks.
2. India must first 'demilitarise' the region.
3. A third country should monitor the talks.

The erstwhile People's Front government headed by Radhabinod Koijam offered, on February 28, 2001, a unilateral month-long cease-fire, commencing March 1 to March 17, 2001 with the Indian State. Subsequently, on March 19, 2001, Governor Ved Marwah announced the setting up of a contact group to liaison with extremist groups in the State. However, the initiative was failed without any development (Sahni: 2002). Again on January 31, 2005, UNLF had come up with a four-point formula to resolve the armed conflict in Manipur. There was no positive response from the government. The claim that they will honour the wish of the people. The Four points are:

1. A plebiscite under United Nations (UN) supervision to elicit the opinion of the people of the State on the core issue of restoration of Manipur's independence.
2. Deployment of a UN peace-keeping force in Manipur to ensure the process is free and fair.
3. Surrender of arms by the UNLF to the UN force, matched with the withdrawal of Indian troops.
4. Handing over of political power by the UN in accordance with the results of the plebiscite.

RPF and its armed wing PLA have reaffirmed its stand not to have a political dialogue with the GOI except on the issue of independence and sovereignty of Manipur after their second congress (July 14 to December 4, 2008) resolution. The armed militancy among the Meiteis continues unabated even as of now. The Naga and the Kuki group are now negotiating with the government (Table 2.5).

Nagaland

The Naga national movement is basically an ethnic one wherein the Nagas struggle to constitute an independent nation-state for

Table 2.5: Annual Fatalities in Armed Conflict in Manipur, 1992-2009

Year	*Civilians*	*Security Force Personnel*	*Resistance Group**	*Total*
1992	84	30	51	165
1993	266	91	66	423
1994	189	98	63	350
1995	183	64	74	321
1996	117	65	93	275
1997	233	111	151	495
1998	87	62	95	244
1999	89	64	78	231
2000	93	51	102	246
2001	70	25	161	256
2002	36	53	101	190
2003	27	23	148	198
2004	50	41	127	218
2005	138	50	143	331
2006	107	37	141	285
2007	150	40	218	408
2008	131	13	341	485
2009*	53	6	240	299
Total	**2103**	**924**	**2393**	**5420**

Source: The South Asia Terrorism Portal (*www.satp.org*).
Note: Data till August 31, 2009;
* The suspects who mostly turn out to be civilians were clubbed under Resistance Group by the database. It leads to denial of any assistance from the State.

themselves, that is, for the several ethnically related tribal groups which had come together and recognized themselves as 'Nagas' or 'Naga'(Vashum: 2005). It is still contentious who are Nagas and which areas they represent but it is generally accepted that the British popularized the term since the early nineteenth century. It is supported by the fact that the communities in Manipur which were recognized by their tribal names were later included into the Naga fold and some of them are leading the movement even though their communities were not involved in the crucial period of the movement. Prof. Kamei (1996) observed that the Naga national feeling or the Naga nationality is a product of British colonialism, the Second World War, of modernization and the Naga movement of political sovereignty. However, the evolution of Naga nationality is not a *fait accompli* but an ongoing search for ethic identity. The present day Nagas of

Manipur, Nagas of Arunachal, Assam have a very different historical evolution with the Nagas of Nagaland.

A pan Naga movement, however, can be traced only from the early twentieth century after many Nagas witnessed the First World War in Europe when they served as part of the British Army. The battle of Kohima against the Japanese forces during the Second World War was also a major inspiration to the Nagas. It is from this period mainly that the Nagas tasted the meaning of nation-state. Accordingly, in 1918, a Naga club was formed by the village headmen, government officials and those who returned from the war. It provided a platform for the Nagas in Naga Hills to discuss their political future and thus led to the concept of Naga nationhood (Roy Burman J.J.: 2008). Religion particularly Christianity has played a crucial role in evolving the Naga nationhood (Baruah: 2005). In 1929, the Naga submitted a historical memorandum to the Simon Commission in Kohima, wherein the Nagas demanded for excluding them from the proposed 'reformed Scheme' of India, and leave them alone like they were before. Despite the plea, the Naga Hills district was merely clubbed as an 'Excluded Area' in 1937 (Vashum *op. cit.*).

It can be noted that the signatories of the memorandum were from the Naga Hills particularly Angami (15 out of 20) and interestingly a Kuki of Naga Hills was also the signatory while the so-called Nagas from Manipur were not. Among the signatories there were 9 *dobashis* or interpreters, 3 teachers, 2 clerks, 1 doctor, 1 *potdar*, 1 treasurer, 1 sub-overseer, and 1 *chaprasi*. The institute of *dobashis* was instituted by the British in the Naga Hills as in the rest of India. *Dobashis* were mostly village chief or erstwhile chief. Given the context of the memorandum submitted to the Simon Commission which appeal to keep the Nagas out of modern political institutions and process and permit them to retain their old tribal structure, and given the background of the *dobashis* who were really in chief in reality, it is like that these chiefs feared the loss of power, privilege and hegemony which included economic assets if a new political system was imposed on them and their appeal was only an attempt at preserving the *status quo* (Nag: 2002).

Naga nationhood took a more decisive turn when the Naga Hill District was created in 1945 under the guidance and initiatives of British Deputy Commissioner, Mr. C.R. Pawsey. It was renamed as Naga National Council (NNC) in February 1946. It became the federation of several tribal councils with proportional representation of one member for every 10,000 people. Initially, it had 29 members but there was no representation from the Nagas of Manipur. It also published a monthly newspaper 'Naga Nation'. NNC did not speak of separation from British India in the beginning but things changed in the late 40s. T. Aliba, Secretary of the NNC observed that it would be 'unwise' for the Nagas to cut themselves off from India at this stage. The Nagas could press for 'protection' against the fears and apprehension and secure 'Home Rule' under Indian administration. Since the debate over identity and future of the Nagas was still continuing and the fear of alien rule still persisted, the Naga elites wanted a time to resolve these issues themselves. They wanted a ten-year interim arrangement at the end of which the Nagas could decide if they wanted to merge with India or otherwise (Nag: 2002). So in February 20, 1947, NNC sent a Memorandum to Lord Mountbatten, then the Viceroy of India for setting up an 'interim government' for the Nagas but the idea did not work out.

This event was immediately followed by the 'Hydari Agreement'. The preamble of the agreement recognized the right of the Nagas to develop themselves according to their freely expressed wishes, under which the agreement, all cases whether civil or criminal arising between the Nagas in Naga Hills will be disposed of by a duly constituted Naga representative's organization. The government interpreted this agreement as that the Nagas have only the power to suggest revisions of the administration powers after ten years. But it was not accepted to the extremist Naga leaders like Phizo who felt that it was a sell out especially due to the last clause. The moderate groups led by Aliba Imti and T. Sakhire were happy with the agreement. In order to resolve the issue between the NNC, Mr. Charles Pawsey, the British DC stationed at Kohima asked the NNC to put the issue to vote. The moderate group led by Aliba Imti and T. Sakhire won by a majority and subsequently Phizo withdrew from the NNC and formed the 'People Independence League for Sovereign Nagaland'. He started mobilization for the movement but could not win much support and Phizo was left with no alternative but to return to the NNC. On his return he successfully lobbied for his ideas (Nag: *op. cit.*).

A seven-leader delegation was sent to New Delhi to pursue the Naga cause but unfortunately they could not meet any of the interim government members. This agreement became the point of contention between the Nagas of Naga hills and Government of India. It is believed that the situation in Naga hills was appraised to Mahatma

Gandhi by the Naga delegation. It is reported that Gandhi said, "the Nagas have every right to become independent. We don't want to live under the domination of the British and they are leaving us. I want you to feel that India is yours. I feel the Naga Hills is mine just as it is ours. But if you don't want to join the Union of India nobody will be forced to do that (Roy Burman: 2008). But the source of the text is still contentious. No Indian leader who are close to Mahatma ever confirmed the reported statement. Mr. Pyare Lal, Secretary of Gandhiji, later denied the contention of the Naga leaders about the statement (Kotwal: 2000).

Not satisfied by the political development, the Nagas in Naga Hills declared independence on 14th August, 1947, one day before Indian independence. Phizo took the leadership of NNC and declared plebiscite in 1951 on Naga Independence which lasted for about two months. It was reported that 99.99 per cent of the people voted for independence. 1952 and 1957 elections were boycotted. Civil disobedience movement was started and tribes refused to pay tax to the government. The plebiscite in Naga Hills cannot be considered as the voice of Nagaland as Tuensang area was later included as a part of Nagaland. The Nagas of Manipur never participated in any crucial activities of Naga Hills even during the plebiscite, civil disobedience movement as well as boycotting of election. Instead, the Nagas in Manipur joined the electoral politics and were elected to the Parliament. In 1953, Nehru's visit to Nagaland was turned out to be a humiliation. The Nagas protested the visit for refusal of their demand to read out a statement at the public meeting; for the acceptance of the nine-point programme and conceding their rights to secede after ten years (Vashum: 2005). Following the incident, the government arrested many Naga leaders, tortured innocent people and terrorized the masses. In 1954, armed violence escalated under the leadership of Phizo and many of the NNC leaders who were against the violent way resigned from the NNC. The Naga Home Guards and Naga Safe Guards were formed for the purpose of armed resistance under the leadership of Thungti Chang and Kaito Sema.

In March 22, 1956, the Nagas in the meantime organized their underground outfits and formed the Federal Government of Nagaland which hoisted the Flag at Pheninyu, A Rengma village. Constitution "Yehzabo" was drawn up. It has a Parliament of 100 MPs (Tatars); President (Kedahge); 15 Cabinet Ministers (Kilonser); Governors of various tribal areas; Magistrate; Deputy Magistrate and other related officials were appointed. The two armed groups were merged to form the 'Naga Country Guard' on 8th November, 1956. It was later changed to Naga Home Guards and finally to Naga Army on 3rd January, 1964 (Vashum: 2005). Those who were against the system of NNC were all eliminated including the former secretary of NNC, Mr. Sakhrie. NNC increased the activities of armed violence to make their claim for the Naga right to self-determination but the government responded by imposing Armed Forces Special Power Regulation, 1958, which later spread to the rest of North-East by renaming it as Armed Forces Special Power Act (AFSPA) 1958. Subsequently, human right violations by the security forces have become rampant. Out of the 861 villages existing in those days, 645 villages were burnt down by the Indian Security Forces in the year 1955-56. Similarly, more than one lakh Nagas died from bullets, aerial bombardment, torture, murder, rape, starvation and disease (Iralu: 2005).

The military campaign in the form of air force and ground forces compelled Phizo to move out of Nagaland in order to work out the future course of action and to seek international support for the movement. He managed to escape to East Pakistan on 6 December, 1956 and by June 1960, he was in London to lobby for the movement. The government successfully co-opted some of the moderate leaders of NNC and started negotiation after Phizo's exit from Nagaland. The Naga Peace Convention was formed and through its negotiation (16-point agreement), the Nagaland State was inaugurated in 1963 but it did not satisfy the extremist group of NNC. The architect of the Naga Peace Convention and subsequently to Nagaland State Dr. Imkongmeren was murdered in 1961. A Naga Peace Mission was formed in 1964 under the leadership of Jayprakash Narayan but it was wound up with no development of the situation. It was failed because the negotiation of the Peace Mission was more particularly with the Indian Union. The FGN leaders rejected any offer short of complete Independence and a sovereign Nagaland. At this point, the Naga underground was seriously afflicted by factionalism within its ranks. The Tatar Hoho blamed Kughato Sukhai for failure of the talks, and he was forced to resign as Prime Minister of FGN. The change in NNC leadership brought inter-tribal rivalry between two groups, the Angamis and the Sema, to the fore and resulted in a series of assassinations organized by both sides. A revolutionary group emerged from within the ranks and the two factions indulged in fratricidal warfare during this time. Finally, the

Semas formed the Council of Naga People, unilaterally dismissed "the Angami-dominated FGN", and constituted Revolutionary Government of Nagaland on November 2, 1968 (Das: 2008).

The moderate group of NNC formed an organization called "Nagaland Nationalist Organization" and decided to abandon violence and signed a peace treaty with the Government of India in 1975 which is popularly known as 'Shillong Accord' (Table 2.6). This move was not accepted by Phizo. It was reported that the pro-Shillong groups formed its own militia called 'People's Militia of Nagaland (PMN), and in fighting among the groups lead to formation of Naga Socialist Council of Nagaland (NSCM) under the leadership of Muivah, Isak Chishi Swu and Khaplang in 1980. But soon the NSCN witnessed friction mainly on the issue of tribal affiliation, leadership and the future of Nagaland. The situation became so critical that it led to gun battle between the two groups and suffered a rift and as a result two parties were formed in the late 80s. One led by Khaplang—a Hemi Naga from Myanmar (NSCN-K) and other by Issac-Sema Naga (Nagaland) and Muivah—a Tangkhul from Manipur as (NSCM-IM). NSCN (IM) was admitted to the Unrepresented Nations of People's Organization (UNPO) in 1993.

NSCN as part of its strategy is playing the role of forming several ethnic insurgent organizations in the region particularly in every State. They support mostly the small and ethnic based groups in training and gathering arm and ammunition. It is learnt that 70 per cent goes to NSCN (IM) and 30 per cent for the host organization. For instance, they support Hmar People's Convention (HPC), Dimasa National Volunteer (DNV) of North Cachar Hills, Assam, Achik National Volunteer Council (ANVC), and Hynniewtrep National Liberation Council (HNLC) of Meghalaya, Zomi Revolutionary Front, and Kanglei Yaoul Kanna Lup (KYKL) of Manipur, National Liberation Front of Bodoland (NLFB), Bodo Liberation Tigers (BLT), Karbi National Volunteer (KNV), Dima Halim Daoga (DHD), National Liberation Front of Tripura (NLFT). It also supports the Muslim based People's United Liberation Front (PULF) of Manipur, Muslim United Liberation Tigers of Assam (MULTA), etc. The purpose is to open up multi fronts for the counter-insurgency agencies like police, army intelligence, etc., and to keep them busy elsewhere rather than concentrating in the strongholds of the core insurgent group. In addition to this, it helps the core insurgent group to mobilize additional resources from areas beyond its sphere of influence as well as provide

Table 2.6: Roadmap to Peace in Nagaland

Sl. No.	*Year*	*Actor*	*Demand*	*Result*
1.	20th February, 1947	NNC to British	Interim Government	—
2.	May 1947	NNC to Bordoloi Committee	Interim Government	—
3.	June 1947	NNC and GOI	Interim Government	Hydari Agreement
4.	1957	Church leader without the consent of NNC	Peaceful settlement	
5.	1957, August 22-26	Moderate NNC	Resolve within Indian Constitution	All Tribal Naga People's Convention
6.	1958, May 21-23	—	—	Second People Convention
7.	1959, October 21-23	—	—	Third People Convention
8.	July 1960	—	Sixteen Point Agreement	Nagaland State was created
9.	1964, January 31-February 2	Council of Nagaland Baptist Churches (CNBC)	Peaceful settlement	Peace Mission was created
10.	1975, November, 10-11	Church	Peaceful settlement	Shillong Accords
11.	1992, January 2	Council of Nagaland Baptist Churches (CNBC)	Peaceful settlement	—
12.	2002	Council of Nagaland Baptist Churches (CNBC)	Peaceful settlement	—
13.	August 1997	NSCN and GOI	To bring a long lasting solution	Still going on

Source: Compiled by Author.

the necessary cover-ups for its operation in an altogether different ethnic-social milieu. The formation of the United Liberation Front of the Seven Sisters (ULFSS) in 1993 and Self-Defence United Front of the South-East Himalayan Region (SDUFSEHR) on November 30, 1994 is worth mentioning. Since ULFSS is not working so they started SDUFSEHR to begin the coordination (Kotwal: 2000). It includes most of the small ethnic based organizations of the region supported by NSCN(IM).

The factional fights have become the order of the day in the name of Naga Sovereignty. Due to ideological differences within the NSCN (IM), a group was formed in the name of NSCN (Unification) group comprising members mainly from Nagaland and was supported by NSCN(K), but they were heavily attacked by the NSCN(IM). The fall of Naga National Movement was because of the clash of ideologies—Communism, Christianity, native Naga doctrine. Mall (2008) observed that, they wish to be a devout Christian to please the Christian countries; they want to prove that they are also a staunch follower of communism (Maoism) to please China; they do not want to antagonize Hindus as well because they will starve without the help of Hindustan. At the same time, they wish to preserve Naga identity. Under these circumstances, they change their colour more swiftly than a chameleon (Mall: 2008—*The Morung Express*).

Table 2.7: Strength of Active Outfits in Nagaland

Outfits	*Approximate Cadre Strength*	*Weapons and Explosives*	*Area of Influence*
NSCN-IM	2000-2500	A.K series rifles, LMGs, UMGs, Grenade launchers, IEDs.	Phek, Kohima, Tuensang
NSCN-K	1,000-1,250	A.K series rifles, LMGs, UMGs, Grenade launchers, IEDs.	Dimapur, Makokchung
NNC	250-500	AK series Rifles, locally made weapons	Phek, pockets of Tuensang, Makokchung and Wokha

Source: Routray (2009).

The main forces of the NSCN(IM)—the Tangkhul of Manipur were the most discontent among the Nagas of Nagaland. The Nagaland Youth Liberation Front (NYLF) was formed in 1990 to counter the NSCN(IM) and on many occasions the NSCN(K) served 'quit notice' to Tangkhul to leave Nagaland. The Nagas of Manipur were considered as 'Impure Nagas' as they were not part of the crucial phase of the movement. Initially, Nagas of Manipur particularly the Tangkhul was not included into the Naga fold while Nepali, Kacharis, Kukis, Abors, Karbis, Khamtis and Sinphos were included. Today Muivah is leading his movement (NSCN-IM), in ethnic cleansing of the Kukis forgetting that one of the Kukis signed the memorandum to Simmon Commission as a Naga (Kumar: 2007). According to Bhaumik, Naga insurgency can be broadly classified into four broad phases:

1. 1957-64 : Intensified Guerrilla Warfare in Naga Hills.
2. 1964-75 : Movement reaches its peak and also was weakened after split.
3. 1975-1987 : NNC split and NSCN emerged.
4. Post-1987 : NSCN split on tribal lines to NSCN (IM) and NSCN (K).

We can add one more phase of Peace Talk (1997 onwards). The NSCN (IM) is on a peace talk since 1997 without any visible development of peace. The ceasefire between the NSCN (IM) and Government of India was extended to Naga Inhabitants areas of North-East in 2001 which lead to strong reaction from the States of Arunachal, Assam and particularly Manipur. It was considered as a design to achieve the dream of "Greater Nagaland". But the government had to withdraw and delete the word "without territorial limit" and confined to Nagaland. Justification for the extension of cease fire was drawn from the 1964 cease fire which was extended to Ukhurl, Mao and Tamenglong. But the cease fire was mostly done for military operation and/or to please the Naga Hill leaders. This can be observed from the fact that the Naga of Manipur stuck to the stand of remaining with Manipur instead of acceding with Nagaland. The All-Tribal delegation went to Delhi in May 1970 for demanding statehood of Manipur (Koireng: 2007).

Another development is that, the NSCN(IM) has given up the idea of sovereignty and Government of India has promised to incorporate a chapter in the Constitution of Indian detailing about the Naga special status. They also have agreed to the presence of Indian Security Forces and to control over Nagaland foreign relation—it only expect Government of India if Nagaland interest is involved. But the road block for settlement remain with Muivah's insistence of integration of Naga-inhabited areas of North-East India. However, the Government of India has not accepted the demand for 'Greater Nagaland' (Bhaumik: 2007).

The peace treaties that have been signed make little sense as the extortion by the underground group is ubiquitous. This also leads to infighting among the Nagas themselves. Even though NSCN (IM) have addressed the United Nations and opened office in many countries, they are also similarly involved openly in State election of Nagaland and Manipur. The NSCN(IM) supported Democratic Alliance of Nagaland and made alliance with Bharatiya Janata Party (BJP) during the last election and there are seven BJP MLAs in the State Assembly. The issue is that BJP is an avowedly orthodox Hindu party which professes the "one nation, one state" policy. NSCN(IM) on the other hand publicly states that it wants nothing sort of full sovereignty. They even denounce the pattern of Sami Parliament (Roy Burman: 2008).

In Manipur, NSCN(IM) supported United Naga Council to nominate candidates in all the hill districts except Churachandpur for the last General Assembly Election. The idea of greater Nagaland was the main forces behind this process. It was a challenge for the NSCM(IM) whether people of the hill districts whom they believe to represent really accept them or not. All this process was conducted in a well organized meeting at Senapati district with participation by all the Naga leaders of Manipur and Nagaland. The election result shows that NSCN(IM) ideas of greater Nagaland were not much accepted by the people in the hills districts of Manipur. They won only in Ukhrul district—birthplace of Muivah and surprisingly they managed to win only one seat in Tamenglong, Chandel, and Senapati. It is reported that forces were used to those who acted against it. Candidates were kidnapped by the NSCN(IM). The recently concluded Lok Sabha Election (2009) of Manipur where NSCN(IM) sponsored outer (hill district) candidate Mani Charinamei, champion of Greater Nagaland, but he lost with huge margin. Takhul Naga Long—the highest socio-political body of the Tangkhul also presented a memorandum to make Ukhrul as a summer capital of Manipur to the Cabinet Secretary, Mr. Pillai on his recent visit to Manipur (Thohe Pou: 2009). So the idea of Greater Nagaland seems to be vested interest for few influential Nagas of Manipur particularly Tangkhuls. Presently, a number of marginalized tribes of North-East want to be included in the Naga fold partly as they find the five decades old Naga movement for recognition inspiring (Roy Burman: 2008).

Though overwhelming majorities of the Nagas do not question their past and the basis of formation of their nationhood, the Naga leaders of the Congress Party published a pamphlet countering the popular feelings. They wrote: "The stark and inescapable truth is that neither did we have a definite and unified political structure and nor did we exist as a nation. We were actually a group of heterogeneous, primitive and diverse tribes living in far-flung villages that had very little in common and negligible contact with each other...Each village was practically an entity in itself. The main contact between villages was through the savage practice of headhunting. Mutual suspicion and distrust was rife. Internecine warfare was the order of the day. There was no trust or interaction between different tribes. In these circumstances, the question of a unified "'Naga nation' did not arise" (Nagaland Pradesh Congress Committee). B.K. Roy Burman (1988) observed that "Many Nagas were unaware that race and religion by themselves do not unify people into a nation. In that case China and Japan should not be fighting one another in the 1930s and 1940s. The whole of Europe should have one nation... further, it is to be kept in view that the localized other ethnic groups in the adjoining countries, who have cultural similarities with the Nagas, are at different levels of technological development, have different traditions of political organization and have been involved in the affairs of their respective nation-state in diverse manner" (Table 2.8).

Assam

The Bodos or Kacharis were one of the original inhabitants of Assam. The Ahoms, who ruled for about 600 years, migrated from Shan in upper Myanmar/Burma in the thirteenth century and a kingdom was founded by prince Sukapha who was the brother of King Maulang—a powerful ruler of Shan Kindgom. After arriving in Khamjang in Assam, Sukapha and his men tried to appease the tribal inhabitants, mostly Morans and Barahis, in eastern part of the valley by marrying the native women. Later, they conquered different parts of Assam valley and established the Ahom Dynasty in Assam. There were many small tribal kingdoms in Upper Assam before the advent of Ahoms like the Baro-Bhuyans, Chutias and Kacharis. Ahoms assimilated the

Table 2.8: Annual Fatalities in Armed Conflict in Nagaland, 1992-2009

Year	*Civilians*	*Security Force Personnel*	*Resistance Group**	*Total*
1992	34	33	29	96
1993	62	43	68	173
1994	110	26	56	192
1995	80	25	108	213
1996	144	48	112	304
1997	104	38	218	360
1998	26	14	72	112
1999	26	4	118	148
2000	13	4	84	101
2001	25	2	76	103
2002	5	2	29	36
2003	3	3	31	37
2004	35	1	22	58
2005	9	0	31	40
2006	10	1	81	92
2007	20	0	88	108
2008	42	2	101	145
2009*	7	0	5	12
Total	**755**	**246**	**1329**	**2330**

Source: The South Asia Terrorism Portal (*www.satp.org*).

Note: The suspects who mostly turn out to be civilian were clubbed under Resistance Group by the database. It leads to denial of any assistance from the State.

* Data till August 31, 2009.

local people by accepting Hinduism, learning the local language and also by following their customs and tradition which helped them to consolidate their power in Assam. With the request from Ahom king in the eighteenth century, the British assisted the Ahom Kingdom to eliminate their opponents. But, in later years the Myanmar/Burma intervened on the pretext of support their friends in Assam. In the early nineteenth century, Myanmar forces occupied Ahom Kingdom and the Ahoms sought help from the British again to throw the Myanmarese forces. The Anglo-Burmese/Myanmar war broke out in 1824. The war was carried out simultaneously in Assam, Cachar, Manipur, and in Burma/Myanmar itself. The British won the war which led to the signing of Treaty of Yandaboo in 1826. The British which had already explored the rich natural resources of Assam in their earlier visit formally closed the glorious history of Ahom dynasty by introducing the British rule. Assam formally became a part of British India (Tarapot: 1994). The Kingdom was about 500 miles in length, with an average breadth of 60 miles. The above limits had remained stationary since 1892 when the Moghuls were expelled from Lower Assam, and the old western boundary of the Manas River resorted. The Ahom Kingdom of Assam thus roughly corresponded to the five districts of the Brahmaputra Valley Division—Kamrup, Darrang, Nowgong, Sadiya and Lakhimpur, and portion of the Sadiya Frontier Tract. Present day Assam is made up of these districts plus the Goalpara region and minus the Sadiya Frontier Tract which has become part of Arunachal (Bhuyan cited in Misra: 2005).

The British occupation of Assam brought certain major changes both in terms of administration as well as economy. The boundary of Ahom was expanding gradually to include most of the areas of present North-East except the State of Manipur and Tripura. As the British consolidated their hold over the market, trade through the frontier *daurs* or doors gradually petered off and the only major outlet remained the western *daur* or the Hadira or Khandahar chowkey situated at the confluence of the Manas and the Brahmaputra rivers. The Hadira chowkey was abolished which resulted in a sharp rise in the trade with Bengal because of the regular river traffic on the Brahmaputra—the first steamboat being put into service in 1874. Assam-Bengal trade took a new turn with the growth of the tea industry and it occupies the foremost place among the exportable commodities from Assam. The extension of tea cultivation in upper Assam and the operation of coal mines demanded an increase in the import of iron and steel for the laying of the railways. This also led to a large influx of indentured labour to man the tea estates. Thus, by the second half of the nineteenth century, the entire pattern of trade had change, with tea, mustard and jute replacing items like lac, cotton and ivory (Misra: 2005).

But the most significant aspect of the colonial economy was that the people of the region did not benefit much from the "enclave" economy that was being developed by the British. The extracted surplus from the tea industry as well as a substantial portion of the wage bills went outside the provinces and there emerged a serious imbalance between the growing modern sector comprising the tea plantations, coal-mines, oil-fields and the associated infrastructure on the one hand and the near-stagnant traditional agriculture on the other (Guha cited in Misra: 2007). With most of the head offices of the tea companies being located in London and Calcutta, the indigenous sector of the economy may be said to have only marginally benefited by the colonial development pattern. Thus, almost all the expenses related to the tea industry benefited outsiders (Misra: 2007).

The Bengali-Hindus were brought into Assam by the British to work in Assam and serve the East India Company as the native people were not familiar with the British administrative structure and functioning. First, they moved into administrative position, then to modern professions. By the beginning of the twentieth century, they moved into as doctors, lawyers, teachers, journalists, clerks, railways and post office officials, as well as officers of the State Government. At the same time, Bengali-Muslims, mostly cultivators from the present Bangladesh, had also started migrating to more fertile land of Assam (Tarapot: 1994). Thus two major demographic changes took place during the year 1874-1905: (a) a shift in the ethnic composition of the population; and (b) a change in its spatial distribution over the districts. Non-indigenous elements came to constitute at least a quarters of the population of the Assam proper in 1901 (Guha cited in Misra: 2007). In addition, (1) it created pressure on land, (2) caused unemployment to the Assamese people claiming themselves as native to the region, (3) decreased the native Assamese percentage *vis-à-vis* the immigrants both in consecutive censuses and electoral roll and, as a result, (4) fomented social tensions that often have ignited ethnic and communal riots (Das cited in Das Samir Kumar: 2007).

The influx of foreigners into Assam was in two phases, i.e., pre-independence and post-independence phase. The pre-independence phase started in 1826 and further subdivided into 1826-1905 and 1905-1947. In the first period, the influx pertained to three classes of people—tea plantation labourers from Bihar and Orissa; Office employees from Bengal who came with the British administration and tradesmen from Rajasthan and Bengal. Then in 1905, Bengal was partitioned and a separate province of East Bengal and Assam was established. This triggered the influx of Muslim peasant from East Bengal into Assam who began settling in the rural areas. Though the partition was annulled in 1912, it continued till 1947. The second phase began in 1947. A large number of Bengali-Hindus migrated to Assam during partition. Even after the partition the influx continue, and by 1963, millions of people from East-Bengal and Nepal have settled in Assam while the land mass of Assam was shrinked by the creation of Nagaland, Mizoram, Meghalaya (Singh Col. Rajinder:

2009). The 1911 Census Commissioners wrote that the migrant was to destroy more surely than the Burmese/Myanmar invaders of 1820. According to one estimate, by the end of the nineteenth century 4,00,000 migrant's labourer had produced 145 million pounds of tea in the region. Between 1911 and 1921, the tea industry brought in 7,69,000 labourers, and another 4,22,000 migrated in the following decade. The 1931 Census indicated 14,00,000 tea garden labourers in Assam (Weiner 1978 cited in Rajagopalan: 2008). As a precaution, "Line System" was introduced in 1916 to curb illegal migrants. An imaginary line was drawn to segregate areas where new immigrants could settle from those which were declared as the "exclusive preserve" of the Assamese people (Rajagopalan: 2008).

When the Cabinet Mission was in India to develop the interim government, Andrew Clow, the Governor of Assam presented that Assam has always maintained distinct identity and this must be preserved in the future Constitution of India in the form of a separate State. Simultaneously, Sadulla, a Muslim League leader and former Chief Minister of Assam, presented that Assam was a Muslim majority province and, therefore, it should be incorporated in the proposed state of Pakistan. Failing to arrive at a scheme acceptable to all parties, the mission suggested a three-tier federal system wherein areas such as defence, foreign affairs, communication were to be vested in the centre. Section A was allotted to Hindu majority, B and C to Muslim majority in the north-west and north-west of the province. Since a full-fledged Pakistan seems impossible, this scheme provided M.A. Jinnah with a choice of opting for a united country where the Muslims would have a majority in both north-west and north-east. In case of partition, Assam had the danger of being transferred to Pakistan. Even in the alternatives scheme it was not only clubbed with the Muslim majority provinces but was also with Bengal which it dreaded. Both the schemes were not acceptable to Assamese leadership and in their fight against the scheme; they sought the support of the tribals to strengthen the case. Assam premier Gopinath Bordoloi appraised that the future of Assam was in the hands of the tribal, if the tribal promise to opt for India after independence Assam could be retained in India. Together with the tribal, the Hindus would outnumber the Muslims thereby thwarting the Muslims' claims that Assam was a Muslim majority Provinces. And it was only in a secular and federal India that the future of the tribal was secure (Nag: 2002).

The immediate impact of the partition on Assam and the North-

Eastern Region was that it was cutoff from the rest of the country. The most convenient rail route through East Pakistan/Bangladesh lay disrupted and the river route was no longer operational. The traditional trade and communication routes died down. It took almost a year for the rail link with the rest of India to be restored through the 'Chicken Neck' 21 kilometres Siliguri Corridor. Trade and communication suffered badly because of the absence of a proper communication network, industrial infrastructure. The province's economic woes were compounded by the large-scale flow of refugees from newly created East Pakistan, the almost incessant migration of poor peasants and after-effects of the extractive colonial economy of the British (Misra: 2007).

The large influx also affected the economy of Assam and created chronic of problems of unemployment and underemployment. Ecology too was affected. The Bangladeshis and Nepalis reside in the prohibited lands near forest, disturbing the ecological balance. These changes gave rise to resentment and frustration among the indigenous people. The official response to these concerns of the people was indifferent and mute. The 'Immigration Expulsion' of 1950 was not implemented and was repealed in 1957. The 'Passport Act' of 1951 was also not put into effect. Truly speaking, the immigrants were serving as 'vote bank' of some political master and as such the post-independence election arithmetics of some parties encouraged this (Singh Col. Rajinder: 2009). By 1961, 60,000 Bengalis were already settled in Assam (Bhaumik: 2007). As a result of the population movement from Bangladesh, minorities are said to be deciding factor in as many as 40 of 126 Assam State Assembly Constituencies (Das Samir Kumar: 2007). Recent enumeration of electors list in Assam by the Election Commission shows more than 30 per cent increase in 17 Assembly constituencies and more than 20 per cent increase in 40 constituencies between 1994 and 1997. Assam has the average growth rate of 16.4 per cent between 1994 and 1997 whereas the All India average growth rate is 7 per cent (Sinha: 1998).

Not only the Bangladeshis but the Nepalis are also of similar concern. The Nepalis (Gurkha) after their retirement from the Gurkha army were encouraged by the British to settle in the foothills, forest fringes and other strategic locations on the frontier thus creating compacts of Nepali settlement in North-East States. This was probably because the British wanted their own stocks of Gurkhas rather than to rely on Nepal all the time. Many of the retired Gurkha soldiers after their retirement also took up dairy farming, agriculture and cattle

Table 2.9: Relative Decadal Percentage Growth of Population of Assam, All-India and Bangladesh

Year	*Assam*	*All-India*	*Bangladesh*
1901-1911	16.99	5.75	9.10
1911-1921	20.48	–0.31	5.40
1921-1931	19.91	11.00	7.06
1931-1941	20.40	14.22	17.60
1941-1951	34.98	21.51	0.10
1951-1961	34.95	24.80	29.83
1971-1981	23.80	24.66	31.83
1981-1991	23.80	23.85	22.00

Source: Sinha (1998).

grazing. The migrant were seen as a threat to their identity and opportunity. Prof. Monirul Hussain observed that 'irrespective of their length of stay in Assam virtually become dangerous unwanted foreigners, who were threatening the socio-cultural and political identity of the Asamiyas in their traditional homeland' (Nath: 2005) (Table 2.9).

Initially though the tribals raised the issue, the Assamese mainland was relatively peaceful. But since the late 1970s when the saffron parties raised hue and cry about the Bangladeshi Muslim, the entire State got engulfed into a cauldron of violence (Roy Burman: 2009). The situation in Assam became acute after a tribunal setup by the Chief Election Commissioner, detected 45,000 voters as foreigners in Mangaldoi Constituency of Darrang district. The magnitude of the presence of foreigners in one constituency shocked the people of Assam. This gave birth to the Assam Agitation, which was super headed by "All Assam Gana Sangram Parishad" (AAGSP) which was formed on 27th August, 1979, All Assam Student Union (AASU), and Asom Sahitya Sabha (ASA). AAGSP was essentially a political mouthpiece of All Assam Student Union (AASU). It soon spread its tentacles allover Assam, particularly the Barahmaputra Valley (Singh, Col. Rajinder: 2009).

The movement leaders had spelt out that the issue of citizenship of foreigner could be decoded on the basis of the National Register of citizen of 1931 or the Voters List of 1952. But this has been ignored deliberately by concerned authorities which bound to agitate the public mind. The currently landmass Assam as per 1901 census had a population figure of 3.1 million. If we consider the all-India population growth factor of 13 per cent annual increase, its population should have been 12.43 million and not 26.6 million as the 2001 Census reveal. Out of this, the Muslim population today is 30.9 per cent which was barely 8-9 per cent in 1950. This abnormal increase is primarily due to influx of outsiders, which has affected the demography of Assam. And on the other hand is the decreasing of landmass, from 2,24,600 in 1912 to its present of 78,000 square kilometres (Singh Col. Rajinder: 2009).

During the Assam agitation, some militant organizations like Assam Fighters' Union, Assam Matri Mukhi Bahini, Jagriti Matri Mukti Bahini and Assam People's Liberation Army came into being and they gave a 'militant' turn to the agitation (Tarapot: 1994). The United Liberation Front of Assam (ULFA) was formally constituted on 7th April, 1979 at the deserted Rang Ghar pavilion in Sibsagar, once the seat of the Ahom Kingdom. It was formed under the leadership of Rajiv Konwar, better known as Arobindo Rajkhowa; Golap Barua, also known as Arup Chetia; Samiran Gogoi and Paresh Baruah with the objective of liberating Assam through Armed national liberation struggle from the clutches of the illegal occupation of India and to establish a sovereign Independent Assam. ULFA supported the boycott of poll of 1983 by AASU and AAGSP until the names of illegally settled "foreigners" were deleted (Das: 2007). But recently ULFA remained soft with the migrants from Bangladesh as Bangladesh became a safe heaven for the ULFA leaders. In a lengthy pamphlet entitled ULFA's call to the groups from East Bengal living with Assam (Asombasi purbabangeeya janagoshthiloi ULFAr Ahum), redefines the concept of "the Assamese" (Asomiya) as "a people of all communities, the mixture of people who are determined to work for all-round progress of Assam". However, the ULFA's call alienated the middle class who were in the forefront of the movement (Das Samir Kumar: 2007).

ULFA began developing network with another like-minded organizations after the 1983 election especially the Assam People Liberation Army (APLA). The APLA was formed at the same time as ULFA by Arpan Bezboruah in the city of Tezpur. The two groups merged formally by signing an agreement in 1985. ULFA utilized the network of APLA's channel as part of their strategy of liberating Assam by merging the two organizations. Most of the ULFA cadres were drawn largely from the ranks of AASU. AGP regime came to power in 1985 were reportedly "hand in glove" with them. ULFA was given a free hand and was declared illegal only on November

27, 1990 (Hazarika: 1995). The delay in announcing ULFA, unlawful even after ten years of existence reveals the close relation with the ruling AGP. This close relationship was due to the fact that AGP, AAGSP, and ULFA owe their common origin to the Assam movement. They instrumented in winning the election both in 1985 and 1996. During the initial year, ULFA theory of denationalization by building a strong trans-ethnic solidarity as a bulwark against the colonialism was not accepted by many communities. The theory was replaced by "combined nationalism of all the exploited people of Assam". It called for the self-development of each nationality, including the Bodos settled in the northern banks of Brahmaputra in the region known as Independent Assam. Sajal Basu observed ULFA's nationalism is territorial and not ethno-linguistic (Das Samir Kumar: 2007).

The first army operation was launched with the objectives of "liquidating" ULFA in 1990 named as "Operation Bajrang". It was closely followed by "Operation Rhino" in 1991. ULFA was declared illegal and series of armed operation was launched against it. Pressure from the business interest appears to be a significant factor behind the government's decision to strike against ULFA. This is revealed in the government action after the killing of eminent industrialist Surrendra Paul. First, it decided to relocate the top management cadre of tea companies facing threat for ransoms from ULFA to safe haven. In the early hour of November 8, 1990, Indian Air force troops were involved in air-lifting top executives of Brook Bond, Lipton from the airstrip controlled by aviation research centre, which worked under the auspices of the Research and Analysis Wings in Tinsukia (Das Samir Kumar: 2007).

Since the 1992 the security forces indulged into indiscriminate mass arrests, tortures, mass killing, rapes and other gross violation of human rights. The entire Upper Assam became a virtual military camp with both the judiciary and civil administration becoming immobilized. During 'Operation Bajarang' around 50,000 troops were amassed by the army in Assam.Vilages in Upper Assam were combed by armoured personnel carrier as well as helicopters to provide cover. In spite of the military setback and significant loss of political standing, the violence perpetrated by ULFA continue strongly. The government also succeeded in splitting the ULFA and ensured surrender of many ULFA cadres. The surrendered ULFA leaders or the SULFA cadres were provided with weapons to liquidate the ULFA members (Roy Burman: 2009) (Table 2.10).

The SULFA provide information to Indian security forces about

Table 2.10: Strength of Active Outfits in Assam

Outfits	*Approximate Cadre Strength*	*Weapons and Explosives*	*Area of Influence*
ULFA	700-1000	A.K series rifles, LMGs, mortars, pistols, grenade launchers, Chinese grenades, sniper rifles, TNT and RDX	Dibrugarh, Tinsukia, Sibsagar, Karbi Anglong, Dhemaji, Nalbari, Sonitpur, Kamrup
KLNLF	150-200	Locally made rifles, AK series rifles, pistols, Chinese grenades	Karbi Anglong, North Cachar Hills
DHD-Black Widows	150-200	Locally made rifles, AK series rifles, pistols, Chinese grenades	Karbi Anglong, North Cachar Hills
MULTA	50-100	Locally made rifles, AK series rifles, pistols, Chinese grenades, explosives	Dhubri

Source: Routray (2009).

ULFA, and they even went to Bhutan to attack ULFA and its members were used in the brutal killing of ULFA relatives and sympathizers like local editor Parag Kumar Das, who has emerged as an ideologue of the movement. Many of its leaders like Swadhinata Phukan, were liquidated in prison or in fake encounters. And the SULFA was provided huge money from "secret source fund" of the army and the intelligence agencies and their leaders were provided with lucrative business deals like the control of the coal trade on Assam-Meghalaya border. Many SULFA leaders now figure among Assam's new billionaires. Indian intelligence used mercenaries or surrendered militants to attack ULFA leaders like Paresh Baruah in foreign countries. The ULFA also responded in similar measure and terror tactics as used by the Indian intelligence but it begin to lose out public support after the 2004 incident in the northern town of Dhemaji (Bhaumik: 2007).

Government of India offered peace talk to ULFA immediately after the first army operation as well as the second operation in 1992 but they did not work out as the Paresh Burua expressed his "dissatisfaction" with the "unconditional surrender of arms" and "one-sided acquiescence to the Constitution of India" as per the terms of the talk (Table 2.11). In December 2003, ULFA headquarters in Bhutan was stormed and a number of its top ranking cadres were killed and many arrested. Noted writer Indira Goswami initiated the peace process in 2004 but ULFA initially rejected the offer of the government. Goswami seems to have convinced the government to discuss the issues of sovereignty. In an interview with Nava Thakuria, she observed that *"the issue of sovereignty* per se *should not be seen as a precondition... I understand that the [Prime Minister] will have to find out some middle path and some solution after consulting all parties and experts. However without the sovereignty issues, the ULFA leaders are unlikely to come*" (Thakuria cited in Das: 2007).

To start negotiation, an eleven-member People's Consultative Group (PCG) comprising mainly of the well known civil society activist was set up by ULFA. After making thirteen round of talks, ULFA insistence on sovereignty led to the break down of the talk in 2006. The continuation of Army operation during the talks that killed at least thirty six ULFA cadres by the security forces also contributed to the breakdown of talks (Table 2.12). Although peace dialogue has been deadlocked, the government has not ruled out the possibility of holding peace dialogue even at the height of army operation. After the recent

Table 2.11: Roadmap to Peace in Assam

Sl. No.	*Year*	*Actor*	*Demand*	*Result*
1.	Mid-1990	GOI	Negotiation for peaceful settlement	ULFA rejected
2.	1991	GOI and ULFA	Negotiation for peaceful settlement	Fail
3.	12th January 1992	Section of ULFA	Negotiation for peaceful settlement	ULFA work out
4.	July 1996	ULFA	Sovereignty and Independent Assam	Fail
5.	1999	ULFA	Negotiation for peaceful settlement	Fail
6.	2004	Prof. Indira Goswami	Negotiation for peaceful settlement	Progress
7.	19th November, 2004	Prof. Indira Goswami	To initiate dialogue on ULFA demand for Sovereignty	Progress
8.	Early 2005	Prof. Indira Goswami	To work out a peaceful settlement	11 members People Consultative Group was formed.

Source: Compiled by Author.

army operation began, then—Home Secretary observed: "Let them [ULFA] come for talk". As Army former Chief J.J. Singh pointed out: "the Army has been given an assignment to perform. If we can compel them to come to the negotiating table and abjure violence, the peace and prosperity will come back to Assam. War and peace are inextricably tied together in this game" (Das Samir Kumar: 2007).

Table 2.12: Casualties of Armed Violence in Assam

Year	*Civilians*	*Security Force Personnel*	*Resistance Group*	*Total*
1992	80	34	19	133
1993	74	24	33	131
1994	173	35	63	271
1995	170	73	27	270
1996	302	87	62	451
1997	285	85	167	537
1998	531	72	180	783
1999	214	77	212	503
2000	366	65	327	758
2001	264	59	283	606
2002	138	32	275	445
2003	212	12	281	505
2004	194	24	136	354
2005	149	10	83	242
2006	96	35	43	174
2007	269	19	149	437
2008	224	16	133	373
2009*	129	21	143	293
Total	**3878**	**778**	**2637**	**7303**

Source: The South Asia Terrorism Portal (www.satp.org)

* Data till August 31, 2009.

Note: The suspects who mostly turn out to be civilians were clubbed under Resistance Group by the database. It leads to denial of any assistance from the State.

Tripura

Tripura means 'land besides water'as the indigenous tribes-people of the State call. In Tripura's days of yore, some of its kings controlled large tracts of eastern Bengal. Maharaja Bijoy Manikya is said to have 'taken bath in several rivers of Bengal.' So, Tripura's 'Bengal connection' is no post-partition phenomenon. When the Manikya kings controlled Comilla and parts of Chittagong, Noahkhali and Dhaka divisions of contemporary Bangladesh, they ruled over tens of thousands of Bengali subjects. In 1280 AD, following the submission of Ratna Fa to Mughisuddin Tughril, the Tripura kings first invited many Bengalis of high caste. Many of them were related to the 'Baro Bhuiyans' or twelve warlords of Bengal (cited in Bhaumik: 2002). Historically, three phases of Bengali immigration into Tripura can be identified: the immigration occurring in the pre-colonial and colonial era; immigration caused by the partition upon independence in 1947; and immigration during and following the 1971 session war in East Pakistan/Bangladesh (Adam, *et al.*: 2007).

Tripura is one of the earliest kingdoms in eastern India. It is believed to have been ruled by 185 kings since the establishment of the dynasty some 5,000 years back. Presently, the State has an area of 10,491 square km with an approximate population of 3.19 million (2001 Census). The landmass of Tripura was much bigger before merging with India in 1949. It includes the present Tripura and the plains of Tripura (Tippera). Plain Tripura comprise of Chakal Roshanabad which was a revenue rich area but it was included in East Pakistan after the partition. It was almost disconnected with other parts of India because of the partition as most of the railways network passes through East Pakistan. It was followed by large wave of refugees flow from the East Pakistan. The sudden pressure of huge influx coupled with the withdrawal of communication network became a big obstacle for the economic development. Tripura has experienced the three forms of people's displacement arising out of human related pressure: (i) displaced in another country and entering a State like Tripura; (ii) displacement within the States of the same nation; (iii) displacement inside (Saha: 2007). The decadal growth rate of population was as high as 78.71 in 1951-61.

The Manikya kings of Tripura also encouraged the Bengali migrants to help, organize and maintain the structure for modern administration and also for the 'jungle-avadi leases', so as to initiate settled agriculture cultivation in order to boost royal revenues. They started gathering momentum from the beginning of the twentieth century. In Hill Tipperah, since the end of the nineteenth century, they accounted for more than 40 per cent of the population and the tribe people were barely in a majority. Even in the normal course of migration, the tribes-people would have become a minority in Tripura.

But Partition opened the floodgates and speeded up the process. In just two decades, the tribal were reduced to a decisive minority (Bhaumik: 2002).

After the partition, the Bengali dominated State Government allowed thousands of Bengali refugees into core tribal areas of 1,950 sq. miles as Tribal Reserve earmarked by King Bir Bikram as a Tribal Reserve in 1943. But in 1948, the Regent Maharani's Dewan A.B. Chatterji threw open 300 sq. miles of this reserve for refugee settlement, often bearing names like 'Atharacard' (Eighteen Cards) or 'Baiscard' (Twenty-two Cards) after the number of card-holding refugee families. Because of this policy, the tribal were marginalized as foreigners in their own land (Bhaumik: 2002). But some scholars observed that the migration from Chakla Roshanabad—earlier part of Tripura Kingdom should not be treated as migration. According to them, it was an internal displacement rather than migration from foreign country. They also argued that tribals never enjoyed absolute majority—though they constituted 47 per cent of the total population of Tripura in 1941-51. But in the later decades, the Bengali population outnumbered them. In 1981, the tribals were reduced to 29 per cent of the population. In 1991, due to the faster growth of tribal population, they constitute 31 per cent and the Bengali 69 per cent of the total population (Saha: 2007).

Table 2.13: Decreasing Tribal Population in Tripura

Year	*Total Population*	*Percentage Variation*	*Total Tribal Population*	*Percentage of Tribals*
1874-75	74,523	—	47,523	63.77
1881	95,637	28.33	49,915	52.19
1891	137,575	43.85	70,292	51.09
1901	173,325	25.99	91,679	52.89
1911	229,613	32.48	111,303	48.47
1921	304,347	32.59	171,610	56.37
1931	382,450	25.63	203,327	52.00
1941	513,010	34.14	256,991	53.16
1951	639,028	24.56	237,953	37.23
1961	11,42,005	28.71	360,070	31.50
1971	15,56,342	36.28	450,554	28.95
1981	20,53,058	31.92	583,920	28.44

Source: Bhaumik (2002).

The tribal lands have been alienated to the refugees. By the 1960s, indigenous tribal had lost more than 60 per cent of their land to immigrants. The main factor of ethnic upsurge is due to the massive influx of refugees from Bangladesh (cited Roy Burman: 2009 forthcoming). In response to the marginalization of the tribal, Sengrak (literary meaning clenched) emerged in the late 1960s to protect against the rampant and systematic grabbing of tribal lands encouraged by the Bengali Dominated Congress Government. It led to the formation of Tripura Upajati Juba Samiti (TUJS) in June 1967 with the main objectives: (i) formation of autonomous district council for tribal, (ii) extension of inner-line regulation of Tripura, (iii) introduction of "Kokborok" in Roman script as medium of instruction for tribal students, (iv) restoration of alienated tribal lands. Similar Tribal National Volunteers also emerged. In 1978, the initially 400 strong Tripura National Volunteer (TNV) emerged as a more radical cell within the TUJS (Adam, *et al.*: 2007).

Table 2.14: Strength of Active Outfits in Tripura

Outfits	*Approximate Cadre Strength*	*Weapons and Explosives*	*Area of Influence*
NLFT-B	30	Locally made rifles, A.K. series rifles, Chinese grenade.	West and Dhalai district
ATTF	200	Locally made rifles, A.K. series rifles, Chinese grenade.	West district

Source: Routray (2009).

Unprecedented ethnic strife broke out in June 1980, engulfing the entire State. Nearly 350 Bengalis were killed in one night on 5th June, 1980. It was followed by unprecedented ethnic riots in which more than 1000 people, mostly Bengalis died. The whole of State was under curfew for more than one year. More than 1,20,000 Bengalis have been displaced and 6,000 plus died due to guerrilla attacks and frequent massacres since 1980 (Bhaumik: 2000). After one decade of violence, TNV-group under the leadership of Bijoy Hrangkhal, returned to normal life after an accord with the Government of India. This led to factionalism within the TNV and TUJS that eventually results in the formation of National Liberation Front of Tripura (NLFT). NLFT aims to carry out the "unfinished agenda" of "freeing Tripura from India's subjugation". It is ironical that the militancy in Tripura does not show any sign of remission—despite accords and efforts by the State Government. On the other side, the drama of surrender and rehabilitation of tribal militants continue and on the other, newer extremist outfits are born (Saha: 2005). Between, 1995-2003, 2000 abduction cases were reported to the police. Many of those kidnapped failed to return even after the families paid ransom. Expectedly, Bengalis have started hitting back through the United Bengal Liberation Front (Bhaumik: 2000). The conflict between the son of the soil and other still continues even today.

Table 2.15: Annual Fatalities in Armed Violence in Tripura, 1992-2009

Year	*Civilians*	*Security Force Personnel*	*Resistance Group*	*Total*
1992	59	18	21	98
1993	148	28	7	183
1994	206	22	10	238
1995	178	34	45	257
1996	140	31	18	189
1997	205	50	19	274
1998	214	25	26	265
1999	240	41	22	303
2000	453	16	45	514
2001	239	31	42	312
2002	94	43	38	175
2003	195	39	61	295
2004	66	38	63	167
2005	34	8	31	73
2006	11	19	30	60
2007	10	5	21	36
2008	7	4	16	27
2009*	0	0	1	1
Total	**2499**	**453**	**516**	**3465**

Source: The South Asia Terrorism Portal (www.satp.org).

* Data till August 31, 2009.

Note: The suspects who mostly turn out to be civilians were clubbed under Resistance Group by the database. It leads to denial of any assistance from the State.

Mizoram

The advent of British rule have somewhat altered the socio-economic structure of the Lushai Hills. The British sought to modernize the Lushais through the introduction of Christianity, Western education, modern hygiene, medicine. As a result, a middle class emerged which naturally became the leader of the Lushais. The Young Lushai

Association (YLA) in 1930 was formed under the initiatives of the church. It was a socio-cultural organization which worked for the welfare of the people. YLA was renamed as Young Mizo Association (YMA) to broaden its membership. The Mizo society can be broadly divided into two groups, the minority Sailo chiefs who ruled over the majority of the commoners. The Mizos were not only bearing oppression under the British but also under the chiefs who had the supreme power over the rest of the society. The autocratic nature of Sailo chiefs is worth mentioning. The British administration recognized the chiefs' council which had 22 elected chiefs and conferred greater power to them. During the Second World War, the chiefs were made to fight against the Japanese. The British support for chiefs can be seen from the fact that they rejected the demand of the commoners for greater representation to the District Council as they were in majority. The minority chiefs had 20 while the majority had only 23 seats.

The Mizo Commoners Union was formed under the initiatives of YMA on 9th April, 1946 but later known as Mizo Union—the first political party in Lushai or Mizo Hills. It was recognized as the only organization for the Mizos living in North Eastern India. Sajal Nag (2002) observes that Mizo Union was significant in three major aspects. Firstly, it united most of the large and small sub-tribes and clans under one generic category. Secondly, it integrated the stratified Mizos society into one whole, e.g., the division between the chiefs, his favourites and the commoners were to be placed on equal footing. Thirdly, the Mizos were now provided with a platform of their own through which they could meet the impending crisis. The Mizo Union became popular in the neighbouring areas. NNC Secretary General, T. Sakhire participated in the Mizo Union Conference in 1946. Khasi leader Rev J.J. Nichols Roy who was a Cabinet Minister in the Gopinath Bordoloi Ministry of Assam invited the Mizo Union leaders for discussion in Shillong.

When the British were departing, the Mizos along with the other tribal areas had the option to join India, Pakistan or remain Independent. Simultaneously, the Cabinet Mission recommendation to evolve constitutional devices to protect the rights and interest of the minorities and tribals, resulted in the formation of the Bordoloi Committee or North-East Frontier (Assam) Tribals and Excluded Areas on 27th February, 1947. Initially, there was no Mizo representation as promised to Mizo Union but later two members were co-opted. On the other side, on 5th May, 1947, a pamphlet written by D. Rongkhaka, "Zoram Independent", was distributed in Aizawl, persuading Mizos to declare independence. Subsequently, on 5th July, 1947, United Mizo Freedom Organisation (UMFO) was formed under the leadership of Lalbiakthanga, an ex-Burmese Mizo military officer. They believed that it would be difficult to talk of an independent Mizoram after 15th August, 1947. So Mizo Hills along with the Mizo inhabited areas should be unified before the boundaries between India, Pakistan and Burma was demarcated. UMFO wanted to merge Mizoram with Burma. But it soon faded away as UMFO is described as 'Party of the Privileged' and mostly supported by chiefs, the people wanted to get rid of.

Since the Constituent Assembly was set up to frame the Constitution of free India, participating in it implied consenting to be part of Indian mission. Due to this reason the Nagas who had joined the Committee, later withdrew from it as they decided not to join the Indian Union. But the Mizos remained with the Committee. In early 1947, Mizo Union was split into two parties on the issue of leadership. When the Committee visited the Mizo Hill, both the parties submitted separate memorandums to the Committee. The right wing represented by Pachunga and Vanlawma demanded maximum autonomy within the jurisdiction of India. The left wing was in favour of joining India provided the interests of the tribal were provided with constitutional safeguards. They even demanded the unification of all the Mizo inhabited areas under one administrative unit and setting up a National Council with an independent judiciary, legislature and executive. But both parties insisted on a ten years arrangement following which the Mizos would have the right to self-determination. The former was anti-India, pro-chief and pro-British while the latter tended to be militant, anti-chief, and an integrationist organization. Most of the leaders of the latter party were from outside the Mizo hills and strongly advocated the integration with India. They were able to win over the people because of their policy of anti-chief and thus consolidated as representatives of the Mizo people (Nag: 2002).

Mizo District Council in October 1958 predicted the imminence of famine on the basis of the Mizo calendar and cycle, following the flowering of bamboos and passed a resolution that the State administration takes precautionary measure. The Mizos named this unusual occurrence after the name of a bamboo species. One is called Mautam, the other is called Thingtam. Mautam and Thingtam occur periodically at interval of every 50 years. The past occurrences are as follows: (i) Mautam-1862; (ii) Thingtam-1881; (iii) Mautam-1911; (iv) Thingtam-1911; (v) Mautam 1959; (vi) Thingtam-1977; (vii) Mautam-2007. On the basis of the recommendation, the Council requested the State Government to sanction a sum of Rs. 1,50,000 relief money to be spent on Mizo district including the Pawi-Lakher region. But the Assam Government rejected the request dismissing the prediction of famine as a tradition of 'primitive people' (Nag: 2002). The famine hit Mizo Hills and even the government could not respond effectively. Thousands of people died of starvation. The Mizo National Famine Front (MNFF) was formed in September 1960 in order to render voluntary service to the affected people. The MNFF become more popular than the Mizo Union as Mizo Union supported the Assam Government and could not influence the Assam Government to help the affected people. The introduction of Language Bill which forced the non-Assamese to learn Assamese created further discontent.

This created lots of frustration and on 28th October, 1961, MNFF reorganized itself as Mizo National Front and was converted to a political party with Laldenga as the President. MNF was elected to the State Assembly as well as village council with absolute majority (145 out of 228). The difference between the Mizo Union and MNF was sorted out through a conference at Churachandpur (Manipur) in January 1963. The conference resolved MNF to drop demand for secession from Indian Union and also to integrate all the Mizos areas of North-East into one administrative unit. Meanwhile, the MNF had prepared itself for a *coupd'état.* They trained its cadre under the Mizo National Army which was formed on 22nd October, 1961. After mobilizing more than five years, about 800-1300 MNF took the government by surprise (operation Jericho) on 28th February, 1966 by a violent attack which continued up to 1st March, 1966. The action took place simultaneously in Aizawl, Chawngte,Chimluang, Champai, Demagiri, Kolasib, Lunglei, Saireng and Vairangte. They disrupted the communication system including the highways to prevent Indian Army from coming to Mizo Hills. On 1st March, 1966, the MNF declared unilateral independence and set up a parallel government in exile with Laldenga as the President of Mizoram (Nag: 2002).

The security forces retaliated heavily. It took more than a month to regain control over the main centres of administration. Indian Air Force was pressed into action on 5th and 6th March, 1966 to eliminate MNF and their position but still MNF had the capacity to resume the armed attacks. A security camp was established on the top of every village to monitor the movements of the people. As a part of the counter-insurgency measure, the army used the anti-insurgency measures learnt from the British and the Americans in Malaya and Vietnam respectively. In fighting the Malayan Peoples Liberation Army in Malaya, British General Briggs has mooted what was known as "Operation Starvation". Its object was to deprive the guerrillas of their sources of food and stop them from taking shelter in the villages. Besides imposing restriction on the selling and distribution of food, the army also rearranged the settlements and regrouped the workers so as to check the infiltration of the guerrillas with the settled population. The population was no longer scattered. It was concentrated into units which made it easy to keep strict watch over them. This device was later also tried by the Americans with their strategic hamlets in Vietnam.

Field Marshall Maneckshaw advocated the application of the same in the insurgency areas of Nagaland. Trilok Singh, Member of Planning Commission visited Mizoram in 1966 and approved the regrouping of villages euphemistically called economically viable villages (Nag: 2002). Between January 5th and February 23rd of the following year, 45,107 inhabitants of 109 villages were relocated into different group centres on the main road. The regrouping process continued until 1972 (Das Samir: 2007). Four types of villages were created by the security forces—(i) Progressive and Protected Village (PPV)—the first stage of grouping was done in the early part of 1967 in 19 centres. (ii) New Grouping Centres (NGC)—there were accomplished in the later part of 1967 along the borders of Bangladesh. (iii) Enlarged Loop Areas (ELA)—initiated by the 50th Mountain Brigade operating from Manipur. These were started in 1967 and ended in 1968 along the Manipur-Burma border. (iv) Voluntary Grouping Centres (VGC)—initiated by 61st Mountain Brigade in scattered pockets except the entire southern pockets predominated by Pawi-Lakher tribes (Roy Burman: 2009).

516 villages were regrouped into 110 grouping centres affecting more than 70,000 lives. Grouping of villages severely affected the traditional *jhum* cultivation or shifting hill cultivation. Curfew used to be imposed between dusk to dawn and people were given work permits to go to fields only during the day time. This severely affected the crop output as many people gave up cultivation. The rice production fell from 75,000 tonnes to 35,000 tonnes a year between

1967 to 1972 (Rangaswami: 1978). These affected the social harmony in most villages. There was a rapid rise in crimes like gambling and murder (Nunthara: 1981). In every Group centre, the democratic institutions were virtually withdrawn and administration was initially left to military Post Commanders. Subsequently, Administrative Officers were appointed. Although the Mizos were quite fed up with herding them into concentration camps, very few dared to resist openly (Lalrintluanga: 2009).

When Bangladesh became an independent country, the MNF lost its base as most of its cadres were operating from the then East Pakistan with support from Pakistan Government. Many top leaders including ministers, army chief and about 1,000 cadres surrendered to the district administration and were given amnesty. This had weakened the movement to a great extent and devastated their dream of Independent Mizoram. The regrouping of villages had added with more disadvantages. So by the late seventies, the MNF's resolve to fight had weakened and spate of surrenders from its rank had been engineered by Mizoram's Chief Minister, Thengpunga Sailo—a former Indian Army Brigadier who started a human rights movement in the State and then formed the people's conference that went on to win the elections. The MNF started attacking soft target like "outsiders" from the plains but after a while started negotiations. Laldenga approached the Indian Mission in Kabul to resolve the Mizo problem. The talk could not yield result. Laldenga approached again in 1976 but this time negotiation was successful and an agreement was reached on July 1, 1976, according to which the rebels agreed to abjure violence and continue talks for an amicable settlement. But Laldenga backed out the agreement as some section of MNF protested against the agreement. Laldenga approached again in July 6, 1977 but talk failed after few months in November 26, 1977. He proposed the MNF to lay down arms by January 28, 1978 but the MNF council refused to accept and the talk collapsed and he was arrested. Mrs. Indira Gandhi opened talks with him to resolve the issue in 1979 but his frequent change of demand and attitudes made the government to terminate the talk on January 12, 1982. Thus MNF was declared an unlawful organization and military operation continued. When Rajiv Gandhi became the PM after his mother's assassination, he carried the peace process to its logical culmination by working out a settlement acceptable to the MNF on June 25, 1987. The Mizo Hills was granted statehood and MNF was accommodated in an interim power sharing with the Congress that was ruling at that time (Bhaumik: 2007 and Das Samir: 2007).

Not all are happy with the Mizo Accord that settled the issue of Mizo peacefully. The people outside the Mizo Hills observed that movement was a joint Chin-Kuki-Mizo (CHIKIMS) demanding a Christian autonomous homeland designated promisingly as Greater Mizoram. The non-Mizo CHIKIMS observed that, it was a down-right betrayal literally to their nations who sacrificed their lives, limps and resources for the promised all Christian land. This led to the formation of the Kuki National Front (KNF) under the leadership of Nehlun Kipgen on the 18th of May, 1988 at Molnoi village of Burma, whereas his revolutionary partner Thongkholun Haokip formed the Kuki National Army (KNA) due to ideological and geo-political differences. The KNF was formed to carve out an autonomous Kukiland under the Constitution of India by incorporating all the Kuki settled areas of Manipur whereas the KNA has been fighting for an independent 'Zalengam' which would include all Kuki inhabited areas of Burma, some portion of Ukhrul, Thoubal and Chandel District of Manipur (Kipgen: 2006). The Hmars were unhappy as the demand for Greater Mizoram was not acceded and adjoining Hmar areas were not consolidated. Consequently, the Hmar People's Convention (HPC) was formed in 1986 but it got split into HPC-D. A memorandum of settlement was signed between the HPC representatives and Government of Mizoram on July 27, 1994 which resulted in forming the 'Singlung Development Council'. But HPC-D is still sustaining and has gained support of big organizations—PLA, NSCN (IM). HPC-D joined the People's Revolutionary Alliance (IPRA)—a platform of the five Zo ethnic militant groups: Zomi Revolutionary Front, Two groups of Kuki National Front—KNF-P and KNF-MC, Kuki National Army (Roy Burman: 2009) (Table 2.16).

The Movement in Mizoram has been through three distinct phases: (a) outbreak and peak of intensity during 1966-71. (b) Decline in intensity followed by 1976 Calcutta accord and first split of MNF and soon after followed by surrenders. (c) Sporadic hostile action and periodic negotiation after 1977 leading to the final settlement in 1987 (Bhaumik: 2007).

Classification of Self-Determination Movements in North-East

Bhaumik (2007) broadly classifies movements in India's North-East

Table 2.16: Roadmap to Peace in Mizoram

Sl. No.	*Year*	*Initiator*	*Demand*	*Result*
1.	1971	MNF	Surrender	Amnesty
2.	November 1971	MNF	To solve Mizo problem	–
3.	1974	MNF	To solve Mizo problem	Talk Fail
4.	1976	MNF	To solve Mizo problem	Agreement signed but MNF back out
5.	July 1997	MNF	To solve Mizo problem	Failed
6.	January 28, 1978	MNF	To solve Mizo problem	MNF National Council refused to accept the proposal. Laldenga was arrested
7.	1979	GOI	To solve Mizo problem	Talk failed on 12th January, 1982
8.	1985	MNF	To solve Mizo problem	Mizo Accord signed on 25th June, 1986.

Source: Compiled by Author.

into five categories:

(a) Insurgencies rooted into a deep-rooted historical ethos of independence that developed into a struggle of secession from India—the Naga example is the best and perhaps the only example in this category. In the recent year, NSCN (IM) has climbed down from its demand of secession to one of a "special federal relation" within India.

(b) Insurgencies separatist in rhetoric but autonomist in aspiration, thus easy to co-opt into the so-called Indian "mainstream"—most insurgencies in North-East India like the insurgency in Tripura or the Bodo, Karbi, Dimasa insurgency in Assam.

(c) Insurgency with sharp overtone but one that were ultimately co-opted by the Indian system through sustained negotiation and concession—Mizo insurgency was the best example.

(d) Insurgency seeking to "change the India system" and having linkage with fraternal allies in mainland India—the PLA before 1990 or the communist insurgency of Tripura in 1948-50 will fall in this category.

(e) Insurgency propped up more by one powerful group that continue to function essentially as satellites. The Dragon Force of the United People Volunteer of Arunachal will fall into this category since they are small organization sustained and used as spring boards by larger Assamese or Naga rebel groups to function outside of their own State.

Bhaumik's classification gives an overall idea but misses out some of the important aspects of the movement. His classification is more in line with the movements which have been negotiating with the government. Inclusion of PLA of Manipur as a movement for change of Indian system is problematic as PLA does not fight to change the Indian system like the Maoist in other parts of India. They are trained in the similar ideology but they have stated many times that, they have nothing to do with India and its system. They are fighting for the people of Manipur. This prompts to sign the agreement between the Maoist operating in other parts of India to recognize the "Independent status" of Manipur and to help each other to fight their common opponent—the Indian State. The movements that follow the Nationalist line were missed out like the UNLF of Manipur or the

Table 2.17: Major Militant Outfits Operating in the North-East and their Reasons for Armed Struggle

Sl. No.	*Name of Outfit*	*Cause for Struggle*
1.	United National Liberation Front, Manipur (UNLF)	Independence from India. Forming of Indo-Burma Front
2.	National Socialist Council of Nagaland IM (Nagaland, now called 'Nagalim'), [NSCN]	Earlier: Independence from India. Now: Cooperation with Government of India for a possible solution within the framework of the Indian Constitution
3.	People's Liberation Army, Manipur (PLA)	Independence from India
4.	United Liberation Front of Assam, (ULFA)	Independence from India
5.	Bodo National Liberation Front, Assam (BNLF)	Autonomy within India
6.	Bru National Liberation Front, Mizoram (BNLF)	Autonomy within India
7.	Kuki National Front, Manipur (KNF)	Autonomy within India
8.	Tripura National Liberation Front, Tripura (TNLF)	Loss of identity; fight against illegal migrants
9.	Hmar People's Council, Manipur (HPC)	Autonomy within India

Source: Mentschel, Binalakshmi (2007).

Table 2.18: Ethnicity Based Insurgent Groups

Insurgents organization	*Community Representation*	*Area of Operation*
All Tripura Tiger Force (ATTF)	Tripuri	Tripura
Hmar Peoples' Convention (HPC)	Hmar	Manipur, Assam, Mizoram
Kangleipak Yawol Kanna Lup (KYKL)	Meetei	Manipur
Kuki Liberation Army (KLA)	Kuki	Manipur
Kuki National Army (KNA)	Kuki	Manipur
Kuki Revolutionary Army (KRA)	Kuki	Manipur
Naga National Council (NNC)	Naga	Nagaland
National Democratic Front of Bodoland (NDLB)	Bodo	Assam
National Liberation Front of Tripura (NLFT)	Tripuri	Tripura
Nationalist Socialist Council of Nagaland, Issac-Muivah (NSCN-IM)	Naga	Nagaland, Manipur, Assam, Arunachal Pradesh
Nationalist Socialist Council of Nagaland, Khaplang (NSCN-K)	Naga	Nagaland, Manipur, Assam, Arunachal Pradesh
Peoples' Revolutionary Party of Kangleipak (PREPAK)	Meetei	Manipur
Tripura National Volunteers (TNV)	Tripuri	Tripura
United Kuki Liberation Front (UKLF)	Kuki	Manipur
United Liberation Front of Assam (ULFA)	Assamese	Assam
Zomi Republican Army (ZRA)	Paite	Manipur, Mizoram

Source: Oinam (2008).

Table 2.19: Peace Accords and the Creation and Restructuring of Administrative Units in North-East India

Year	*Accord*	*Parties to the Accord*	*Unit created*
1960	Sixteen Point Agreement	Government of India (GOI) and Naga People Convention	Created the State of Nagaland
1986	Memorandum of Understanding	GOI and Laldenga on behalf of Mizo National Front	Created the State of Mizoram
1988	Memorandum of Understanding	GOI and Tripura National Volunteer	Re-organization of Tripura Tribal Areas Autonomous Council (TTAADC) Promised.
1993	Memorandum of Settlement	All Bodo Students Union President and Government of Assam	Bodoland Autonomous Council
1993	Agartala Agreement/Memorandum of Settlement	Tripura State Government and All Tripura Tiger Force	Renewed commitment to reorganize TTAADC
1994	Memorandum of Settlement	Mizoram State Government and Hmar Peoples' Convention	Sinlung Hills Development Council
1995		Assam State Government and representatives of community orga-nization of the Rabhas, Kabis, Tiwars and Mishings	1. Karbi Anglong District Council becomes Karbi Anglong Autonomous Council 2. Rabha-Hasong Autonomous Council, Tiwa Autonomous Council, and Mishings Autonomous Council which were non-territorial, was established.
2003	Bodoland Territorial Council Aggreement	GOI, Assam State Government and Bodo Liberation Tiger	Bodoland Territorial Council

Source: Rajagopalan (2008).

ULFA of Assam. There are satellite groups operating at the behest of the NSCN(IM) whose main purpose is to divert the attention of the security forces from the core militant groups (Tables 2.17 to 2.19).

Conclusion

The first armed self-determination movement in India's North-East emerged against the forceful merger of Manipur to the Indian union. Force in the sense of overlooking the Manipur State Assembly which was an elected body of the people of Manipur under the Manipur State Constitution 1947; force in the sense of using military might to sign the merger. So it is annexation rather than merger. Legendary leader Hijam Irabot responded by an armed uprising against the merger in 1949 but it was soon crushed by the government. It was quickly followed by Naga National Council in 1956 under the leadership of Phizo for a sovereign Nagaland. The Nagas have started the non-violent opposition by declaring themselves Independent on 14th August, 1947, one day ahead of Indian Independence. The All Manipur Students Union was involved in the mass awareness among the student community of Manipur about the right to self-determination since the late 1970s. The roots for the movement in Assam and Tripura are almost same. The uprising is against the illegal migrants and grabbing the land and opportunities of the natives. While ULFA, UNLF and PLA are still holding on their demand for complete independence from India. NSCN(IM) after ten years of peace talk has agreed to a "special federal relationship". If one looks at how the insurgency started in the States of Assam, Manipur, Nagaland, even though the emergence of the phenomena may vary from one social dynamics to another, one still invariably finds an undercurrent of defiance of a lingering colonial force (Oinam: 2008).

Since the uprising in Manipur, North-East India is continuously militarized. The Armed Forces Special Powers Act 1958 was imposed, which empowers the central security forces to search, arrest and even to kill anyone on mere suspicion with impunity, to suppress the movement which in turn led to massive human right violations and further alienated the people. After four decades, like a nuclear chain reaction, the law has been amended a number of times to accommodate changes in the names and the number of States. It now applies to all of North-East India either partially or fully. The extent of military deployment during the 1990s reveals that there was one armed force personnel for every ten civilians in some parts of the region (Chenoy: 2002).

The expansion of the military and related agencies has created enormous problems for civil society. While the government complains that it has no money with which to support civil institutions, it has pumped millions of rupees every year in the police and the armed forces stationed throughout the State. The security forces who are pitted in a no win situation while fighting the militants, often resort to retaliatory violence on the common people for attacks carried out against the security forces by the militants (Mishra: 2000). The Air Force was pressed to suppress the movement within the so-called Indian Territory, which is an exceptional case but only for the North Eastern Mongoloids people. There are innumerable combing operations and major operations as part of the counter-insurgency operations in this region. Mention can be made of Operation Rhino, Operation Bazrang, and Operation Blue Bird. Operation All Clear (2004), Operation Tornado (2005), Operation Dragnet (2006), Operation Summer Strome (2009) were conducted in Manipur. These operations were remembered by the people and Human Rights bodies because of the rampant human rights violations—especially using villagers as "human shields" to prevent possible ambushes from the militants.

The counter-insurgency strategy of the government is largely influenced by the real politik propounded by Kautilya (also called Chanakya), who helped King Chandragupta Maurya to build India's first trans-regional empire just after Alexander's invasion of India. Kautilya advocated *Sham* (conciliation), *Dam* (Bribe), *Danda* (Forces), and *Bhed* (Split) as the four options of statecraft to be used in effective combinations rather than as single, standards options. If the insurgent groups insist on sovereignty or adopted positions unacceptable to Delhi, military operations were resumed with renewed vigour and intelligence worked overtime to split the recalcitrant insurgent groups. Naga, Mizos, Assamese or other tribal insurgent groups have all ended up with split, mostly during or after dialogue with the federal or the State governments. For instance, The Hmars, the Maras and the Lais fought shoulder to shoulder with the Lushais against the Indian security forces during the twenty years of insurgency led by the MNF. But twenty years of bonding through the shared experience of guerrilla warfare failed to develop a greater "Mizo" identity. The Bodos, the Karbis and the Dimasas all joined the Assam movement to expel "foreigners" and "infiltrators". But after settlement with the Government of India, they felt the Assamese "had taken the cake and left us the crumbs". The result was fresh agitation, often sliding into violent insurgencies, spearheaded by small ethnicities demanding separate homelands. The ethnic imbalance in power sharing has often caused retribalisation, which has had its own cascading effects in restricting the growth of local nationalisms that could challenge the Indian State (Bhaumik: 2007).

It is not that the government of India is not aware of the root causes of the self-determination movement in India's North-East. The Government of India has tried to resolve the Naga issue since the very beginning by signing many peace accords. Similar is the case of the Mizoram, followed by Tripura. The two decades Mizo Movement was the only successful peace accord in North-East India. Presently, most of the ethnic based groups are either into "informal" ceasefire with the Indian army or into peace negotiation with the Government of India at the ministerial level or/are into some forms of bargain. Once ULFA was declared illegal, Government of India invited for peace talk on many occasions without any result. But surprisingly, the resistance group of Manipur like the UNLF, PLA was not invited even once since the beginning of the armed resistance in 1949. The reason may be multiple but one reason may be the legitimate right of the people of Manipur to self-determination, which the Government of India does not want to expose to the international community by initiating a peace talk.

After the creation of United Nations, Self-determination is treated as *jus cogens* and *erma omnes* but the situation is more or less similar with the early twentieth century. Karen Parker observed it as Imperfect Decolonization. Even the UN decolonization process overlooked many of the people and territories which are eligible for exercising right to self-determination. So the United Nations cannot eradicate colonialism if the people and territories which are left out by the United Nations system. The Government of India had been preaching for decolonization all-over the world in every platform but unfortunately the legitimate aspirations of the National Liberation Movements in his own continent are concealed from decolonization. The idea of self-determination need not be seen as inseparable from secession. Secession could be one more among many possible consequent manifestations of self-determination. The lurking anxiety with the State establishment could be overcome if the concept is revisited keeping into account the changes that are happening around the world (Oinam: 2008). Exercising right to Self-determination will be the only way out for a peaceful solution. Suppressing it might be dangerous.

REFERENCES

Adam, J. *et al.*, 2007. "In the name of Father-Christian Militantism in Tripura, Northern Uganda and Ambon", *Studies in Conflict and Terrorism*, 30:11, 963-983.

Ana, Filipa Vrdoljak. 2008. "Self-Determination and Cultural Rights", in Francioni and Scheinin (eds.): *Cultural Human Rights*. Netherlands.: Koninklijke Brill NV.

Akoijam, Bimol and Tarunkumar Th. 2005. "Armed Forces (Special Powers) Act 1958: Disguised War and its Subversions", *Eastern Quarterly*, Volume 3, Issue I, April-June.

Baruah, Sanjib. 2006. *Post Frontiers Blues: Towards a New Policy Framework for North East India*. Policy Studies No. 33, Washington: East West Centre.

Bhaumik, Subir. 2002. "Disaster in Tripura", *Seminar*, No. 510.

Bhaumik, Subir. 2007. *Insurgency in the India's North-East: Conflict, Co-option and Change*. Working Paper No. 10, Washington: East West Centre.

Chandhoke, Neera. 2006. *A State of One's Own: Secessionism and Federalism in India*. Working Paper No. 80. London: Crisis State Programme. London School of Economics.

Chenoy, Anuradha M. 2002. *Militarism and Women in South Asia*. New Delhi: Kali for Women.

Das, Samir Kumar. 2007. *Peace and Conflict in India North-East: The Role of Civil Society*. Policy Studies No. 42, Washington: East West Centre.

Das, Samir Kumar. 2009. "Peace sans Democracy? A study of ethnic peace accords in North-East India", in Sanjib Baruah (eds.): *Beyond Counter-Insurgency: Breaking the Impasse in North-East India*. New Delhi: Oxford University Press.

Halim, Moris. No Date. *Self-Determination: An Affirmative Right or Mere Rhetoric ?*, *http://www.tamilnation.org/selfdetermination/97moris.htm*

Hanjabam, Shukhdeba Sharma. 2008. "The Meitei Upsurge in Manipur", *Asia-Europe Journal*, Vol. 6, No. 1.

Human Rights Watch. 2008. *"These Fellows Must Be Eliminated: Relentless Violence and Impunity in Manipur"*, New York.

Iralu, K.D. 2005. "The fifty-five years of Indo-Naga conflict: A question of internal Indian conflict or conflict between two nations?", in Hussain, M. (eds.): *Coming out of Violence: Essays on Ethnicity Conflict*

Resolution and Peace Process in North-East India. New Delhi: Regency Publications.

Ishay, Micheline R. 2004. *The History of Human Rights: From Ancient Times to Globalization Era*. Hyderabad: The Orient Longman.

Kabui, G. 1996. "Origins of the Nagas", in: Vashum, R. (eds.): *Nagas at Work*. New Delhi: NSUD.

Kamei, Gangumei. 2003. "Ethnicity and Politics in Manipur", Talk on Ethnicity and Politics of Manipur organized by the National Research Centre, at Manipur University on September 16.

Koireng, Singh Aheibam. 2007. *Ethnicity and Inter-Community Conflicts: A Case of Kuki-Naga in Manipur*. New Delhi: Akansha Publication.

Kotwal, D. 2000. "Instability Parameters in Northeastern India", *Strategy Anal*, XXIV (1):137-149.

Kumar, B.B. 2007. "Ethnicity and Insurgency in North-East India", in B.B. Kumar (eds.): *Problems of Ethnicity in North-East India*. New Delhi: Concept Publications.

Maipaksana, Rajkumar.1995. "Constitutional Development in a Nutshell in Peoples Democratic Movement" (eds.): *Annexation of Manipur 1949*. Imphal: Peoples Democratic Movement.

Mall, Jagdamba. 2008. "Factional killings in Nagaland: The Clash of Ideologies", *The Morung Express*, 16th May.

Mentschel, Binalakshmi Nepram. 2007. *Is the Crescent Waxing Eastwards? Pakistan's Involvement in India's North-East and Bangladesh*. Pakistan Security Research Unit (PSRU), Brief Number 14, Department of Peace Studies, UK.: University of Bradford.

Misra, Udayon. 2005. "Assam", in Murayama, Mayumi; Kyoko Inoue and Sanjoy Hazarika (eds.): *Sub-Regional Relations in the Eastern South Asia: With Special Focus on India's North Eastern Region*. Joint Research Programme Series No. 133, (IDE-JETRO).

Mishra, Udayon. 2000. *The Periphery Strikes Back—Challenges to the Nation-State in Assam and Nagaland*. Shimla: Indian Institute of Advanced Studies.

Musgrave, D. Thomas. 1997. *Self-Determination and National Minorities*. Oxford: Clarendon Press.

Nagaland Pradesh Congress Committee. 2000. *Bedrock of Naga Society*. Kohima.

Nag, Sajal. 2002. *Contesting Marginality: Ethnicity, Insurgency and Sub-nationalism in North-East India*. New Delhi: Manohar Publications.

Nath, L. 2005. "Migrants in Flight: Conflict-Induced-Internal-Displacement of Nepalis in North-East India", *Peace and Democracy in South Asia*, Volume 1, No. 1.

Nunthara, C. 1981. "Grouping of Villages in Mizoram: Its Social and Economic Impact", *Economic and Political Weekly*, 16(30): 1237-1240.

Oinam, Bhagat. 2008, "State of the States: Mapping India's North-East", Working Paper No. 12, November, East West Centre Washington.

Parker, Karen. 2000. "Understanding Self-Determination: The Basics", Paper presented to First International Conference on the Right to Self-determination, United Nations, August.

Raic, David. 2002. *Statehood and the Law of Self-Determination*. Hague: Kluwer Law International.

Rajagopalan, Rajesh. 2008. *Fighting Like a Guerrilla: The Indian Army and Counter Insurgency*. New Delhi: Routledge.

Rothermund, Dietmar. 2006. *The Routledge Companion to Decolonization*. New York: Routledge.

Routary, Bibhu, Prasad. 2008. "Northeast: Island of Peace and Ocean of Conflict" in D. Subha Chabdrab and P. R. Chari (eds.): *Armed Conflicts in South Asia 2008: Growing Violence*. New Delhi: Routledge.

Roy, Burman, B.K. 1988. "The Naga Upsurge, Ethnic Identity and Social Change", *Social Action,* 38, January-March.

Roy Burman, J.J. 2008. "Contour of Naga Upsurge", *Asia Europe Journal,* Vol. 6, No. 1.

Sanajaoba, Naorem. 1995. *Right of Oppressed Nations and Peoples.* New Delhi: Omson Publications.

Sanajaoba, Naorem, 1995b. Key Note address to the National Convention on Manipur Merger Issue, in Annexation of Manipur 1949. Imphal: Peoples Democratic Movement.

Sanajaoba, Naorem. 2002. "India's binding obligation to right to self-determination", paper read at a seminar organized at New Delhi by the Lok Raj Sangathan. Retrieved from *http://www.manipuronline.com/Features/March2002/selfdetermination01_2.htm*

Schaeffer, Robert K. 1999. "Secession and Separatism", in Kurtz Lester (eds.): *Encyclopedia of Violence, Peace and Conflict* (Volume 3). San Diego: Academic Press.

Singh, S. Mangi. 1993. "The Manipur State Interim Council", 1947, *The Struggle*, Special Issue, October.

Singh, Karam Manimohan. 1989. *Hijam Irabot Singh and Political Movements in Manipur.* New Delhi: B.R. Publications.

Singh, R. 2009. "ULFA's Niche War", *Indian Defense Review,* Vol. 24.1, January-March.

Sinha, S.K. 1998. "Report on Illegal Migrant into Assam", submitted to President of India by Governor of Assam (Sinha, S.K.).

Tarapot, P. 1994. *Insurgency Movement in North-Eastern India.* New Delhi, Vikas Publications.

Thohe Pou. 2009. "Ukhrul as the Manipur Summer Capital", *http://www.kanglaonline.com/index.php?template=kshow&kid=1687&Idoc_Session=3b9360a4944927fc0acb5b74e858ba23*

Vashum, R. 2000. *Naga's Right to Self-Determination: An Anthropological-Historical Perspective*. New Delhi: Mittal Publications.

3

Ethnic Violence in Post-Independence North-East India

J.J. Roy Burman

North-East India happens to be melting pot of races. Hordes of people have migrated to the region in waves for a very long time. If some have migrated from the east, others have entered from the West. There are evidences to show that people have encroached into the area both from the south and north. The people have not migrated only in the past, but continue to do so even as of now. It is extremely difficult to seal the porous international borders constituting almost 98 per cent of the region linking up with Bangladesh, Bhutan, Tibet and Myanmar.

The periodic immigration and occupation of the territories along with consolidation of control over natural resources have crystallized identities leading to the evolution of ethnic entities along with conflicts between them. Ethnic conflicts in the North-East have now become quite endemic in nature. According to E.A. Henderson (1999: 72) ethnic conflict refers to disputes between contending groups who identify themselves primarily on the basis of ethnic criteria and make group claims to resources on the basis of their collective rights. Ethnic criteria may include perceptions of shared cultures, nationality, language, religion and race. An ethnic group is a collective sharing with a belief in common ancestry, a link with a specific territory (Though not always), a perception of a shared culture, and a belief in a common destiny. The belief in a common ancestry owes as much if not more to myths than to genetics. To be sure, some ethnic communities may result from consanguinal or kinship ties, but to the greatest aspect heritage is a function of belief and not genetic descent ... Myths of common descent are powerful inducements to ethnic identification. Such myths provide symbols around which elites can focus political, economic and social activity. Two factors are among the most significant bases of group identity: belief in a historic homeland and the perception or practice of a shared culture. The latter is often expressed as a shared language, religion, race or customs.

The ethnic upsurge in the North East certainly springs up from the primordial loyalties, but elite mobilization in many of the ethnic conflicts cannot be ruled out. The Assam Movement, for instance, had the support from many different ethnic entities under the leadership of educated elites (Leach, C.W. and Brown, L.M.: 1999).

In the case of North-East, ethnic tussles have been rather intense. Many of the groups like Meiteis and the Nagas have been demanding separate nationhood while simultaneously denying rights to other groups. The Nagas of Manipur resent the attitude of the Meiteis towards them—they are fully discriminated and the government development funds barely reach the hill areas where they dwell.

In the present context ethnic assertions are mainly made by smaller groups who have little power to affirm their threatened identities and retain control over material resources. Their main strategies of resistance depend to a large extent on continued contestation and social anarchy. They continue to struggle against the moves of centralization of power and homogenizing agenda. They stand opposed to the hegemony of the majority community. Many observers believe that ethnic identity politics produce and promote conflict and violence.

Violence in North-East India is not very new. The practice of head hunting was a common phenomenon among the Nagas, Mizos and a number of other tribes in Arunachal Pradesh and Manipur till about 60-70 years back. During inter-village and inter-tribe wars, heads of the enemies were considered as trophies proud to be possessed. The changes in geo-political situation locally and regionally gradually brought an end to the head hunting practices. The Christian missionaries too played a positive role in this regard.

The regimented society—the basis of formation of a warring tribe based on the institution of Age-grade provided the platform of war preparedness. The 'Morung' (Bachelor's dormitories) among Ao Nagas and 'Zawlbuks' among Mizos helped in continuing the feuds.

The regimentation based on Age-grade principles yet exists among most Nagas though the institution of bachelor's dormitory has withered away.

Before looking into the nature of violence perpetrated in the North-East, understanding the concept of violence is imperative. The definition of violence, as per the Oxford English Dictionary (OED 1956-2359) goes far beyond pain and shedding of blood. It is firstly the exercise of physical force so as to damage persons or property, but more importantly for our purposes the forcible interference with personal freedom, violent or passionate conduct or language, passion or fury.

Bates *et al.* (2002) provide some characteristic features of conflict among stateless societies (which is somewhat true for North-East India), "In stateless societies the relevant decision makers are often groups such as lineages and communities. These groups can allocate their resources among economic activities, military activities, and leisure; they are not farmers or warriors at any given time, but rather possess the capabilities of both. Conflict appears to be an ongoing, almost personal feature of many such communities; disputes and potential skirmishes lie under the surface, ready to emerge".

Many scholars have looked upon the concept of violence differently. Wolfgang (1966) writes that violence is a generic term that may include many forms of overt, and often noxious, expressions, ranging from internal physiological changes in the organism of external behaviour that directly impinges upon the safety and security of other organisms. Discord, conflict, protest and even revolution may not necessarily involve violence, as the history of non-violent opposition to established polity and policy has shown.

Violence is generally perceived as the display of behaviour which inflicts physical injury. Not all violence transgresses legal norms, but legal sanctions proscribing many types of violence reflect a general societal opposition to violence, the historical concern with it and the need to regulate its expression.

The nation-states by and large profess the principle of one nation-one state. It tries to homogenize the entire nation. It tries to project a unitary image with common culture base. It strongly defends any revolt or separatist activity (Nagengast: 1994).

Until recently, few anthropologists examined violence and conflict between groups and the state and amongst groups within states, especially violence rooted in ethnicity, nationalism, bids for

In Tripura, the militancy gained prominence mainly due to the tacit support of the communist parties. The militants targeted the civilian population as a part of their strategy to help their patron political parties. Out of the two most criminalized terrorist outfits—the National Liberation Force of Tripura (NLFT) is said to have close link with the ruling Left Front. The Left Front Government has now greatly succeeded in cooling down the tempers and ensure almost total normalcy in the State as of now.

Udayan Misra (2000: 55), a reputed scholar from Assam stated that even the governments of the region have a stake in insurgency as then it can demand for more financial support from the Centre. Kumar (*op. cit.*: 31-32) states that even the bureaucracy in the North-East is in close touch with the militants. They cannot escape from the reaches of the militants who demand ransoms regularly. The Divisional Engineer, Telephones, in Manipur had to pay his life for not waiving the bills of two PCOs operated by NSCN (IM) and People's Liberation Army (PLA). The Chief Engineer, Loktak Project in Manipur was killed by one of the Kuki outfits in January 2000.

It is also apparent that the media and human rights groups in the North-East have also quite often been sympathetic to the militants. They are behind to get support from both India and abroad. The UK based 'Assam Watch', an alleged front of the ULFA, works in U.K. as well as other countries. Assam Watch is said to have sponsored two top ULFA leaders to attend a meeting of the UN Sub-Commission's working group on Indigenous Peoples held in July 1997 at Geneva.

In parts of the country, which are away from the centre and where the State cannot guarantee security of life and property, ethnic militia fill the vacuum. Baruah (*op. cit.*) states that "militant organizations play many roles which the State ought to play...They are more reliable providers of security and more worthy of loyalty than the Indian State. Majority of the militant organizations are ethnically based, even though their political projects are not always exclusionary and may even be pluralistic. The names of some militant groups suggest agendas to liberate homelands, the names of which can be sometimes found on a contemporary map".

The militants in North-East often have bases across the international border in the adjoining countries of Bangladesh, Bhutan, Myanmar and sometimes even in China. Kumar (*op. cit.*: 36) writes that even the ISI of Pakistan imparted trainings. In 1985, the ULFA cadres were facilitated in the camps of Hizbe-e-Islam of Gulbuddin Hekmatyar.

B.B. Kumar (*op. cit.*: 21) views that the militant outfits in the North-East are mainly of three kinds—(i) Secessionist outfit; (ii) Outfits demanding Separate State within India; and (iii) Those demanding Autonomous District Councils. The separatist/secessionist ideologies in the North-East are (1) Ethnic; (2) Ideological/leftist/communist; and (3) Religious. Many militant outfits combine these different traits. The Naga Nationalist Council (NNC) combined ethnicity and religious trait—Christianity and socialism/scientific socialism/communism. ULFA combines ethnic and communist/scientific socialism factors. Most of the Manipuri outfits claim separatist/secession on ethnic (Pan Mongolian/Mongolian/Meitei) and communist ideological ground.

Sahni (Mimeo) classifies the tribal movements in North-East India into three kinds:

1. Tribal groups *vs.* the State;
2. Tribals *vs.* Tribals; and
3. Tribals *vs.* Non-Tribals.

Kumar significantly states that the Nagas do not have common myth of origin and migration. They lack common language, identical social and cultural elements ....To talk of the common memory of the Naga tribes is absurd, as they did not know even the names of the tribes except for the few and had the memory of only the mutual feud and enmity. In the memorandum submitted to the Simon Commission in 1929, names of only eight tribes were included.

Kumar further (*op. cit.*, 24-25) elicits the way the Nagas need to be looked upon. Their country within the administered area consists of more than eight tribes—quite different from one another with different languages which cannot be understood by each other and there are more tribes outside the administered area which are known at present. They have no unity among themselves and it is really the British Government that was holding them together...Naga identity is quite fluid. At one time even Kacharis, Kukis, Abors, Karbis, Nepalis, Khamtis and Singphos were included in the list of Nagas, whereas Manipuri Nagas including the Tangkhul (To which Muivah, the NSCN-IM leader belongs) were excluded from the same. Today Muivah is leading his movement in ethnic cleansing of the Kukis forgetting that one of the Kukis signed the memorandum to Simon Commission as a "Naga."

The NSCN (IM) has emerged as a pioneer militant outfit of the entire North-East. It has helped in the formation of National Democratic Front of Bodoland (NDFB), Bodo Liberation Tigers (BLT), Karbi National Volunteers (KNV), Dima Halim Daoga (DHD), Achik National Volunteers Council (ANVC), and National Liberation Front of Tripura (NLFT). NSCN (IM) is believed to sell arms to these groups and also impart training. It receives 60:40 shares from the collections out of extortions, kidnapping, taxes and robberies (Kumar: 37). Dasgupta (2001) states that the NSCN is the prime vector for proliferation of small arms in the North-East as it has not only access to the clandestine arms market of South-East Asia but also controls the routes through which such arms are smuggled into North-East. ULFA does not lie far behind in distributing small arms and light weapons into the region (Dasgupta: 2001).

The violence in the North-East is presently accounted for not only due to tussle between the security personnel and the militants but also due to fratricidal fights within ethnic outfits themselves. Factional fights are also common between the Bodo outfits—Bodo Liberation Tigers (BLT) and National Democratic Front of Bodoland (NDFB). The keeping out of NDFB during the 2003 agreement has cost the state and the people very clearly. Keeping the Meiteis out of peace negotiations with the Nagas—NSCN(IM) has severely affected the political equations and the State of violence.

A study of thirteen accords in North-East reveals that such accords have failed to ensure lasting peace. Even the so-called successful Mizo accord had to be followed up with two more Accords in the State (Rajagopalan: 2008).

S. Baruah (2007: 9) states that there are several arms groups operating in the North-East, "According to one recent count, there are as many as 109 armed rebel groups in the North-East. In Assam there are 34 rebel groups, two of which are banned; Meghalaya has four rebel groups of which three are active. Mizoram has two active groups. Nagaland has two active and two non-active groups. Tripura has two banned rebel groups, one active group and 22 inactive groups". It is alleged that some of the groups function at the behest of the security forces as counter-insurgency strategies. A study in Nalbari district of Assam revealed that the people are more scared of the security forces than the surrendered militants.

Baruah further states, that one of the main financial sources of the militants is extortion or 'local tax'. It is also evident that the militants thrive more in the poverty-stricken areas.

It is a fact that the militant outfits do not function very democratically. Dissent from the lower ranks is barely tolerated. The leaders also lead a lavish lifestyle. Many leaders have invested huge amounts in industries in Bangladesh and other countries.

Bhaumik (2007) writes that militancy in the North-East has not only received support from the adjoining countries but even the Central Government has played Machiavellian role by propping up the militants to settle scores with the State governments. He, however, writes that the menace of militancy has receded in the last few years. During 2001-05, the fatalities in insurgent action have dropped from 600 in 2001 to 393 in 2005. The negotiations, military success, lessening of public support are considered to be some of the factors for this. Sahni (Mimeo) has also noticed the similar trend earlier. He points out that while the year 2001 saw 606 insurgent related killings, as against 758 in 2000.

At times even the State Governments have been involved in fights against each other. Kindo and Minz (2008) write that on 4th June, 1985, a conflict arose between Assam and Nagaland as a construction of a permanent check gate was in progress in Merapani. The Assam Police objected to it. The Nagaland Police along with armed Naga civilians attacked the Assam Police. The conflict spread out to the adjoining villages. Loss of life and property was high. Ninety six villages involving 7,607 families were affected.

We have extolled certain broad overview of the nature of violence in the North-East in a general way. We will provide the facets of them in a slightly detailed manner covering the different States of the region except Meghalaya and Arunachal Pradesh where the incidence of violence is rather negligible except for certain pockets.

Assam

Ethnic Assamese Upsurge

The State of Assam is a mixing pot of races. Along the fertile banks of Brahmaputra river many alien groups have come and settled for a long time. The lands other than the river bank have been brought under agriculture and tea plantations. The tea plantations have seen the immigration of thousands of tribals from the Chotanagpur region as the local people shied away from plantation labour work. This apart, the State has seen the immigration of thousands of labourers and businessmen from Bihar, Uttar Pradesh and other north Indian States. Apart from these groups, Assam has witnessed the immigration of lakhs of Hindu Bengali refugees after the independence. By 1961, around 60,000 Bengalis were already settled in Assam (Bhaumik: *op. cit.*). The situation became all the more intriguing with the rapid flow of Bangladeshi Muslims during the last many decades. Ethnic Assamese became scared of becoming minorities in their own land.

Along with the flow of immigrants, the ethnic Assamese people felt peeved due to the discrimination meted out by the Central Government. The Centre cheated it by paying less royalty for the oil that it took away. While the State received Rs. 42/tonne as royalty, the centre received six times more. Assam got Rs. 54 as Sales Tax on a tonne of crude oil, Centre collected Rs. 991 on the same quantity. Sales Tax on tea in Assam was Rs. 200-300 million, while West Bengal collected 70 per cent more because the head offices of the tea companies were located there.

In Assam, the ULFA violence was preceded by many forms of non-violent movements like fasting, hunger strike, processions, rallies, marches, etc. But with the coming of ULFA it took a different turn altogether. The Republic Day celebration of 1983, which was boycotted by movement supporters, turned into a blatant display of military muscle against its citizens.

Initially, though the tribal areas throughout Assam and the Brahmaputra valley were in fire for quite some time, the Assamese mainland was relatively peaceful. But since the late 1970s when the saffron parties raised hue and cry about the Bangladeshi Muslims, the entire State got engulfed into a cauldron of violence. According to Bhaumik (*op. cit.*), the situation in Assam turned grim after a tribunal detected 45,000 illegal immigrants in the Mangaldoi Constituency. The Assam Gana Sangram Parishad comprising of several political parties, the All Assam Students Union (AASU) and Asom Sahitya Sabha, stood up together in opposition and started agitating. The agitation against the illegal migrants continued for six years. More than 130 people died during the February 1983 Assembly Elections in Assam. The worst massacre took place at Nellie in Nowgong district where 1600 Muslims were killed.

The agitation acquired a more virulent form with the emergence of United Liberation Front of Assam (ULFA) in 1979. Many anti-migrant agitators joined the ULFA. Some leftist groups like Asam Jatiyabadi Yuba Chatra Parishad (AJYCP) which professes a curious mix of Assamese nationalism and radical Marxism and supports dual citizenship and self-determination, too supported the ULFA. ULFA received a great deal of support from the Assam Gana Parishad (AGP) when it was in power. Many of the ULFA members are ex-AGP and ex-All Assam Students Union (AASU) members. The ULFA made a radical departure from its notion of Assamese and it stated that it stands for 'Asombashis' and not just 'Asomiya'. It acknowledged the positive role played by the Bengali Muslims in the development of Assam. ULFA took to a sort of pro-subaltern stance (S.K. Das: 2007). ULFA initially did not directly attack the security forces, but combined selective terror and parallel tax collection to buildup a support base. With the help of Kachin Independence Party (KIA) and NSCN, ULFA had builtup a standing force of some 2,500 armed fighters by the end of 1990. Slowly it formed a parallel government as well. The main objective of ULFA was to restore Assam's lost sovereignty as it existed at the time of Yandabo Treaty (On February 24, 1826) between the British and the Burmese.

Since the 1990s, the security forces indulged into indiscriminate mass arrests, tortures, mass killings, rapes and other gross violations of human rights. The entire Upper Assam became a virtual military camp with both the judiciary and civil administration becoming immobilized. During 'Operation Bajrang' around 50,000 troops were amassed by the army in Assam. Villages in Upper Assam were combed by armoured personnel carriers as well as helicopters to provide cover. ULFA was declared a terrorist and secessionist organization and banned. During the other assault on the civilians was undertaken during the 'Operation Rhino' in September 1991.

Dasgupta (1997:345-370) states that AASU and AGSP movements were mainly aimed at illegal immigrants. The United Liberation Force of Assam (ULFA) was dominated by educated Assamese (Ethnic) young men. ULFA stood for armed action and violence. Several ULFA cadres undertook military training in Pakistan, Bangladesh, Myanmar and China. It also established links with many other underground outfits active in the region. Significantly, ULFA widened its support base to even non-ethnic Assamese. P. Biswas and C. Suklabaidya (2008: 217-18) state that even as of now the ULFA enjoys considerable support from the peasantry, urban middle classes and the intelligentsia. It identifies the tea garden companies, traders and businessmen as class enemy. Hundreds of prominent businessmen were killed and millions of rupees were levied on businessmen of all kinds. However, the Assamese businessmen, including large tea garden owners were exempted. The political parties like AGP are believed to have supported such ventures. The Assamese people of the Brahmaputra valley too applauded these drives because it supposedly served to recover Assam's wealth for its people. However, the ULFA discourse on national self-determination is caught between the blinds of redefining an Assamese identity and settlement of the question of who is an outsider.

During the height of its prowess, the ULFA cadres stopped the tea plantation workers from working in the plantations. It also intimidated potential candidates from offering their candidature in the elections till the electoral rolls were updated.

ULFA trained its guns against the 'enemies' of Assam—politicians, bureaucrats and others suspected of committing crimes against Assamese society. These crimes could be like drug peddling, prostitution, brewing alcohol, teasing women or exploiting people. ULFA tried to make sure that rural development funds reach the right people. But ULFA started extorting large sums of money from the businessmen and professionals—mainly outsiders. As a reaction, the Hindi speaking Businessmen, Muslim groups and tribal groups formed their own militant organizations to confront the ULFA.

Roul (2007) writes that since the year 2000 the ULFA has killed over 150 Hindi-speaking migrant workers. Thousands of people had fled their homes in Assam to escape the mob and ULFA attacks. The killings began from January 5 targetting mainly the Hindi-speaking brick kiln workers, fishermen and small time shopkeepers in Assam's Tinsukia district. Around 13 villagers were shot dead in fresh attacks on Saturday (January 6) in Sadiya, while on the previous day militants killed at least 19 people, mostly from the State of Bihar, and wounded 25 others in separate shootouts in Tinsukia and Dibrugarh. Sahni (Mimeo) too has noted about the deaths of the Bihari migrants in the year 2000, "16 persons were killed by the suspected ULFA terrorists in two separate incidents in Tinsukia and Dibrugarh districts on October 23, 2000. Another nine were massacred and injured on October 27, 2000 in Nalbari district. On November 16, 2000, ten members of a non-Assamese community were killed in Sibsagar district at a time when a Parliamentary team of Bharatiya Janta Party (BJP) was on tour to monitor the law and order situation in the State. 22 non-Assamese were killed in three separate massacres in Bongaigaon district on November 30, 2000. On December 7, 2000, 28 Hindi-speaking petty traders and farm workers from the State of Bihar were killed by the suspected ULFA terrorists near Sadiya". Prabhakar (2008) too has stated about the continued killings of Bihari migrant labourers in Assam in the recent times. Ahoms attacked Bihari migrants and killed 50 of them. The root cause of this ethnic conflagration was the apprehension that outsiders would grab employment opportunities locally available.

The ULFA suffered serious setbacks due to the emergence of many factions within its flanks. The outfit also suffered due to the successful military operations against it by the security forces in 1990 and 1991.While some of the ULFA adopted a soft posture with India, the others joined the camps in Bangladesh and no longer held the Bengali Muslims as their target. Kumar (*op. cit.*) writes that surprisingly even the Assam Gana Parishad (AGP) wanted to form an alliance (in order to form a government) with the Assam United Democratic Front (AUDF), whose whole agenda is to safeguard, nourish and expand the domain of illegal Bangladeshis and retention of the IMDT Act.

In spite of some military setbacks, and significant loss of political standing, the violence perpetrated by ULFA continued quite strongly. Very often the local cadres and also surrendered ULFA members are involved in such acts (Dasgupta: 1997: 356). In the recent years the fortunes of ULFA have wavered up and down. The public support has tapered down considerably and yet it is able to create a sense of fear through occasional bomb blasts and killings. In 2004 when several students lost their lives during Independence Day celebrations at Dhemaji, a small town, the State witnessed a massive demonstration against the ULFA. The government also succeeded in splitting the ULFA and ensured surrender of many ULFA cadres. The surrendered ULFA leaders or the SULFA cadres were provided with weapons to liquidate the ULFA members.

While a section of the ULFA is interested in having negotiations with the government, the others were opposed to it. The ULFA formed the People's Consultative Group (PCG) to negotiate with the government and still retained the demand for sovereignty. It, however, gave up the conditions to deal through the United Nations and accepted to operate within the framework of the Constitution. But the talks fizzled out in September 2006. However, at present some negotiations are going on through the intervention of Indira Baruah, a noted Assamese literary person and other civil society organisations. Even the Congress Party under the leadership of Tarun Gagoi has made significant article by releasing the ULFA top brass after arresting them (baring Paresh Baruah—the military head of ULFA).

Bodo Upsurge

In response to the ethnic-Assamese chauvinism, many plains tribes of Assam also have taken resort to violence for safeguarding their interests. The Bodo tribes, for instance, consider the Ahoms to be invaders who have promoted the anti-tribal policies since history. Bodos point out the Indo-Aryan antecedence of Assamese language which is different from the Tibeto-Burman affinity of the local tribal languages. Due to the formation of a separate Naga State in 1963, the Bodos got inspired to demand for a separate homeland. They formed the Plains Tribals Council of Assam (PTCA) in 1967 and fought for 'full autonomy' in the plains areas of Assam. In 1971, the Bodos formed a radical students organization called All Bodo Students' Union (ABSU). Under the aegis of the radical groups, in 1973 the Bodos pressed for a separate homeland called 'Udayachal'. The Bodos were extremely scared about their dwindling numbers and demographic features. While constituted 49 per cent of Assam's population in 1947; by the 1971 census they had dropped to 29 per cent due to internal and external migration and the various State restructurings (S.J. George: 1994: 878-892).

The ABSU tried to widen its base and supported the formation of a party called United Tribal National Liberation Front (UTNLF) in 1984. This culminated into the demand for a Union Territory (UT) within the federation for the plains tribal people of Assam in the northern part of Brahmaputra valley. The plain tribes of the South Bank too demanded the creation of District Councils within the provision of Sixth Schedule of the Constitution. The Bodos at that juncture did not take recourse to any violent means and rather collaborated with the AASU and AGP. It is only since the 1980s that the Bodos adopted the hard line. They were opposed to the imposition of Assamese language over them and hence demanded the inclusion of Hindi as the official language and Bodo language written in Roman script for Bodo schools.

The Bodos adopted the strong militant posture only in 1987 after the formation of Bodo Peoples' Action Committee. It was strongly opposed to ethnic Assamese chauvinism promoted by the AASU and AGP. This later on led to the formation of Bodo Security Force (BSF) in 1990. The BSF later changed its name to National Democratic Front of Bodoland (NDFB). The coming of the Congress to power in 1991 did not lead to any significant change in the Bodo outlook. Violence, kidnapping and extortions continued unabated. BSF also established links with the insurgent outfits like ULFA and National Socialist Council of Nagalim (NSCN). The Government of India initiated the 'Operation Zoom Zoom' and provided the Bodo Volunteer Force with arms and explosives and also trained to use them. The Bodos then started attacking the trains and buses to press their demand for a separate Bodo State. Militants also have triggered couple of blasts targeting rail networks and succeeded in damaging a coach of the Rajdhani Express (Bhaumik: 2007).

Bhadra (2007) states that in 1993 as an accord, the Assam Government conceded to form the Bodoland Autonomous Council (BAC). The Council was equipped with its own legislative and executive organs. The Bodo administration was allocated with thirty eight subjects, including matters relating to educational, social, economic, ethnic and cultural affairs affecting the community. The Bodos were, however, not happy as the law and order wing and revenue administration still remained with the Assam State. The BSF militants did not accept the accord. The other Bodo militant organizations like Bodoland Tiger Force (BLTF) which had surfaced in between, resorted to heavy violence, including blowing off trains and bridges. By 1996, Bodo activists had revived their demand for a separate State and violence escalated with the proliferation of militant organizations, including the Bodo Liberation Tigers—BLT (comprising of many surrendered Bodo Voluntary Force members). Many non-Bodo settlers were targeted.

In order to assuage the Bodos, the government in 1993 agreed to start the 'Bodo Autonomous Council'. But this did not assuage the feelings of the Bodos as they did not know clearly the territory and the boundary within the jurisdiction of the Council. Due to the heat generated over this the Bodos indulged in systematic cleansing of the non-Bodo residents in the four districts where they are in majority (the Bodos). Subir Bhaumik (2000) states that the Bengalese—Hindu or Muslim—who controlled the prime agricultural lands and retail business, are the prime targets of ethnic cleansing in the Bodo areas of Assam. But even the 'tea tribes'—comprising of the migrant Santal, Oraon, Munda, etc.—became the targets of the Bodos. In June 1993, between 18,000 to 20,000 belonging to nearly 2,200 families, were affected in the nearby villages. Many flee to the refugee camps and lots of them are yet to be seen living in them.

The third and fourth wave of violence against non-Bodos occurred in May 1996 and May 1998. This time the 'tea tribes' became the main target. They again were compelled to flee to the refugee camps. Sixty-one camps were set up to provide shelter to 1,15,000 riot affected people. Though the tea tribes had tried to retaliate with bows and arrows, they were no match to the sophisticated fire arms used by the Bodos.

Biswas and Suklabaidya (2008) too have recorded the anti-outsider violent movements of the Bodos, particularly aiming at the migrant Muslims concentrated in and around Bongaigaon. They have also noted the attacks on the Hindu Bengalis and the migrant Santals. Das (2007) too states that the Bodos had attacked the Muslims brutally resulting into several deaths. Consequently, the Muslims too had organized themselves and evolved insurgent groups like 'Muslim Liberation Front of Assam' (MULFA).

Subir Bhowmik (*op. cit.*: p. 157) states that the Bodo attacks invited some retaliated later in 1998 and some militant outfits like the Cobra Force formed by the 'tea tribes' killed several hundred Bodos. But the Bodos counter-attacked 2,31,989 tea tribes and they fled into 67 camps in Kokrajhar and 15,238 into 8 camps in Dhubri district.

In May 1980, a new organization—the All Assam Minority Students Union (AAMSU) was formed—which tried to include both Hindu refugees and Muslims. AAMSU demanded that all immigrants who came before 1971 be given citizenship status and harassment against minorities be stopped. During strikes called by AAMSU violence ensued due to opposition by AASU (Baruah: *op. cit.*: 1986: 1184-1206).

In spite, of concerted efforts made by different Bodo underground outfits for the success of their movement, serious differences and factional infights are creating havoc in the Bodoland area of Assam. The main contending Bodo groups are the Bodo Liberation Tigers (BLT), NDFB and Bodoland People's Progressive Front (BPPF). On December 12, 2000, 11 BLT cadres were killed by NDFB in Barpeta district by NDFB. On December 21 again, five BLT cadres were killed by NDFB in Nalbari district. The NDFB resorted to killing BLT cadres once more at Bijni on January 19, 2001. Rahman (2008) in fact, writes that factional clashes between insurgent groups in North-East India are growing intractable with time, and this is leading to ever growing violence that affects not just the peace but also development and economic growth in the region. Work contracts are cornered by people close to the militant groups. Even projects involving small amounts attract the rebel groups for extortion.

Violence in the Karbi Areas

Militancy in Assam is not just confined to the ethnic Assamese predominant areas of Upper and Lower Assam and the Bodo areas. It is also rampant in the Karbi Anglong district and North Cachar hills. Damzen (2008) states that the Karbis have been fighting for statehood for quite some time. Some groups getting frustrated have taken to arms. One of the groups is called KNLF. In the adjoining areas of Manipur the Kuki Revolutionary Army was formed. KRA has its units in Karbi Anglong. These two groups have entered into frequent skirmishes over the areas under the coverage of extortion. The situation got worse as the Kukis banned *jhum* cultivation in the Singhason-Khobamon hills. The frequent fights led to the killing and injuring scores of people. Many people of both sides fled from their native villages to places where their tribes were in majority. Damzen also writes that the fratricidal Karbi-Kuki conflict in 2003 took a toll of more than 120 lives—apart from burning down of more than 1,000 houses in over hundred villages belonging to both the communities. The number of casualties is probably much higher. In March 2004, members of a Karbi militia group allegedly killed six Kuki ginger cultivators who had refused to pay taxes they demanded. In retaliation, members of the Kuki Revolutionary Army—a Kuki ethnic militia, raided three villages and killed as many as 30 Karbi farmers (Samaddar: 2005).

The Karbis feel scared with the sudden influx of Kukis from Manipur and Nagaland and their demand for Kuki Regional Council (KRC). The Kuki community as a whole did not have its own administrative platform to raise their voice in a democratic way. In the Karbi Anglong district the Dima Halong Daoga, a militant outfit, has been active since the 1990s. Their main demand is for creating a Dimaraji or Dimaland for the Dimasa tribe, comprising of North Cachar Hill district and some other adjoining areas of Assam. DHD received weapons and training from the NSCN(IM) in the past. But the agreement between the Nagas and the Government of India about ceasefire has soured up the relations with NSCN(IM).

As North-East has witnessed waves of migration. Tripura became a Bengal-majority area. In Assam, Bengali Hindus and Muslims probably outnumber the ethnic Assamese now. Land was one of the key factors of the movement of the United People's Democratic Solidarity (UPDS)—a rag-tag band of Karbi militants. The killing of the Bihari migrants by the UPDS was avenged by the Biharis with support of the security personnel having similar ethnic (North Indian) affinity. In July 2000, the Black Panthers killed four people in cold blood and another two were murdered by the Hindi speaking migrants at the same time. The killing of the Hindi speaking migrants still goes unabated and in the early 2007 the ULFA killed over seventy of them—mostly brick kiln workers.

Manipur

Manipur is a multi-ethnic State where the dominant Meitei community inhabit the plains valley area and the tribal communities dwell in the surrounding hills. There were many intricate ties between the plainsmen and the hill people that ranged from mutual cooperation to raids and feuds. But Manipur thrived to exist as a princely State till the merger with India (Though in between it was under a notional control of the British). The merger was not a happy episode and the Meiteis consider it to be an Indian conquest. Obviously, ethnic rumblings could be heard of right since 1947.

According to Joykumar Singh (2005: 135) the first armed movement in Manipur after independence was initiated under the aegis of the Communist Party and the Red Guard Army. Irabot Singh was the leader of this movement and many young men joined him (Hanjabam: 2007). The rebels were operating from Keibi. On 18th April, 1950, the Red Guard Army apprehended government spies—two police personnel. They also looted arms from Churachandpur Police Station. On 29th April, 1951, they again attacked the Mayang Police Station in Imphal. This forced the government to place a large number of police personnel in different parts of the State. Being under the government pressure, the rebels set up camps across the border in Burma. But the movement collapsed with the demise of Irabot Singh.

Bhaumik (2007) states that in 1964 a separatist group called United National Liberation Front (UNLF) was formed. But it got split over the issue of revolution. While one of the factions pressed for reforms the other vied for outright revolution. The latter faction called Revolutionary Government of Manipur (RGM) sent many volunteers to East Pakistan (Now Bangladesh) for training. But they did not enjoy full trust of Pakistan and many were sent back to India, only to be arrested by the police.

UNLF was one of the first militant groups formed in Manipur. The leaders went to China and undertook training. They also went to Bangladesh—erstwhile East Pakistan in 1965. The youth volunteers of CONSOCOM, a break away group of UNLF too sent volunteers for training to East Pakistan. CONSOCOM at times indulged in robberies for gaining alms.

The CONSOCOM had formed an underground government called Revolutionary Government of Manipur. There occurred a series of rifts within the party and Bishweshar, one of the founders of the outfit, emerged out strongly with his Marxist linkages. He built some nexus with the Naxalites as well and became the leader of People's Liberation Party (PLA). He came out of the reactionary Meitei chauvinism and developed the Marxism-Leninism—Mao-Tse-Tung thoughts. The RGM gradually became defunct.

The PLA made its intents very obvious by attacking the Police and Security personnel in June 1978. On July 18, 1979, a Bank was looted at Paona Bazar in the heart of the Imphal city.

In 1978, the Revolutionary People's Front (RPF) and its military wing, PLA made contacts with China and undertook military training and ideological indoctrination of 'Marxism-Leninism and Mao Thought'. The RPF stressed on class war and abolition of private property. It opposed sectarian politics based on ethnic or religious appeal. Most of the militant groups in Manipur adopted the urban guerrilla tactics and attacked the security forces and the outsiders. Since 1979, the smaller parties like the Kangleipak Communist Party too followed suit.

The security forces, however, succeeded in penetrating these groups and in 1981 several top leaders were killed or arrested. Bisheshwar Singh, the top PLA leader was arrested. Kunjabehari, the second in line was killed in 1982. Despite the setbacks, the PLA continued with its sporadic attacks on the security forces. The UNLF too followed suit, in spite of a number of splits. In the late 1990, both the PLA and UNLF have emerged stronger. Later, both the groups merged together to form the MPLF. Their strike powers have increased and no longer are they ideologically tied up.

Kumar (*op. cit.*: 31) brings it to notice that the militants in Manipur have been quite potent. At times they have been successful in subverting the public distribution system through their linkages with the politicians. The tankers of kerosene oil, petrol and diesel were diverted from the dealers and sold in black market by all militant groups. Diverted rice from the public distribution system were supplied to the underground camps. The PLA and UNLF sold rice and kerosene at very low rates in the villages close to their camps in Churachandpur and Chandel districts.

The violence perpetrated by the PLA was very professional and civilians were seldom touched. Following the spate violence, the government declared the entire Manipur valley as disturbed area. The Armed Forces Special Power Act (AFSPA, 1958) was promulgated. However, this did not deter the PLA from continuing with its, armed attacks.

The Armed Forces Special Powers Regulation Act (AFSPA), 1958, is an extremely draconian statute, which can permit anybody to be arrested without warrant if he has committed a cognizable offence or against whom a reasonable suspicion exists that he has committed or is about to commit a cognizable offence and may use such force as may be necessary to effect the arrest (Lasuh: 2002: 156). The rape and murder of Manorama Devi by the security forces too was being hushed up citing the AFSPA by the state. Sharmila Chanu, an activist from Manipur has been on a protest hunger strike since November 2000 demanding the report of AFSPA and the withdrawal of the security forces. She was striking in Delhi trying to draw attention of the nation, but she was arrested and removed to a hospital, where she was fed forcibly (Baruah: 2007: 3). In support of Sharmila and the movement against human rights violations 12 women belonging to various organizations protested naked on 15th July, 2004, in front of the Manipur Rifles headquarters. Ironically, in Manipur, certain tribes in the hill areas publicly demanded the continuation of the AFSPA. Inter-tribal-Meitei dynamics is perhaps responsible for this.

In January 1979, the valley witnessed killings and counter-killings, arms and gun-snatching, attacks and counter-attacks for more than a year. Finally, the entire State was declared a 'disturbed' area in 1980. The State was virtually put under Army rule and the people were subjected to army atrocities and not allowed to move freely. Attacks between the security forces and the underground, however, continued everyday.

Up to the middle of 1982, 1,089 extremists and 93 civilians were killed. Rupees 132 lakh were looted. By the beginning of 1985, a group of militants surrendered as 59 PLA members were killed by the security personnel. The PLA had already suffered immensely with the capture of Bisheshwar on July 7, 1981, near Imphal. The splinter groups of the PLA, however, did not discontinue with their armed struggle and made sporadic attacks on the security personnel. Bisheshwar himself formed a democratic party and joined the electoral politics.

In the year 2001, 256 persons lost lives in terrorist induced violence. Of them 70 were civilians, 161 were militants and 25 were security personnel. In the year 2000, 246 persons died for similar reasons.

On August 15, 2003, the Independence Day celebrations were marred by violence as different militant groups attacked civilians and security forces from the early morning. At least eight people were injured. In an incident six people were killed on the spot when the militants targeted a bus full of passengers, when crossing a bridge in Imphal. Two other persons were killed on the same day as they were hit by the militants.

The Indian security has been extremely harsh towards anybody and even the women. The killing of Tangjam Manorama Devi bears a clear testimony to this. She was killed by the Indian Army on July 11, 2004. She was alleged to be a member of the People's Liberation Army. The Assam Rifles stated that she was shot while trying to escape (Budha: 2008). Budha, however, states that violence on women is not a monopoly only of the State security personnel but such crimes at times are perpetrated by the militants as well.

Since 2003, the MNLF and Manipur People's Army (MPA) have effectively thwarted off repeated efforts of the security forces to overrun their main base areas at Sajit Tampak in Chandel and Churachandpur districts of Manipur.

Kuki-Naga Conflict

Oinam (2008: 123) is of the view that the ethnic conflicts have occurred in the North-East just due to loss of control over resources but due to the loss of identity as well, such as apparent in the case of Naga-Kuki, Kuki-Paite or Meitei-Naga clashes in Manipur.

Das (2007) has taken note of the Naga-Kuki conflict in Manipur in the 1990s. According to him in 1993 alone, the conflict resulted into the loss of hundreds of lives and several villages were razed to the ground. A few thousand people were permanently displaced from their homes.

The Kuki-Naga conflict was not restricted to just Moreh town but all-over Manipur wherever the two communities are preponderant. Moreh is a border town in Chandel district where the Maring Nagas and the Thadou Kukis are predominant. On May 12, 1992, the NSCN-IM burnt down Kuki villages of Molphei. Subsequently, on May 30, 1992, the Kuki National Army (KNA) collected an amount of 30,000 Kyats from the Maring villages. On June 3, 1992, some armed NSCN cadres retaliated by attacking a Haokip Kuki village and killed a few people including the headman. In return, the Kukis attacked a few Maring villages of Chandel district. Biswas and Suklabaidya (2008) who have studied the Kuki-Naga conflicts, assail that there are a number of factors responsible for them. NSCN alleges that the Indian Security Forces backed up the Kuki National Army (KNA) initially. But ironically, after a while the KNA attacked the security forces after political shifts. Bhaumik (*op. cit.*) writes that the Indian security forces had come to an understanding with the Kuki and Zomi militant groups in 2005 and drafted them against Meitei rebel groups like the United National Liberation Front.

The main factors of Kuki-Naga clashes in the Chandel district were: (1) Over the control of Moreh, (2) Tax imposed on the Kukis by Nagas, and (3) Refusal to renew the land agreement by the Nagas to the Kukis.

The Naga underground levied many kinds of taxes on the Kuki inhabitants. They divided the people into different categories. Some of them had to pay more than Rs. 3,000 as House Tax. Those who did not pay were either killed or tortured. Cutting and selling of trees were also prohibited. Even if trees were to be felled, the militants had to be informed and paid money. The KNA and the Kuki Federal Council decided to stop paying House Tax to the Nagas and the conflicts ensued. The Thadou Kuki and the Maring Naga conflict in Moreh did not remain restricted locally and it spread all-over Manipur where the Nagas and Kukis lived in close proximity.

Surprisingly Kuki language is taught in a few schools even in parts of Nagaland. Also Kuki language in some places is the common lingua franca between disparate Nagas.

Meitei-Naga Conflict

Conflicts have taken place between the Meiteis and the Nagas in Manipur as well. According to Oinam (*ibid.*) the roots of Meitei-Naga conflict are not limited only to the issues of access to resources and identity but also due to the expansion of the Naga nationalism. Like the Naga, some of the larger tribes are coming out of narrow tribal identity to broader tenets of ethnicity. As compared to a tribe, an ethnic community is more politicised and has a more developed communication network. The inclusion of the Anal, Mayon, Monsang, Maring, Paite, into a common 'Naga' identity is a case in point.

The Meiteis are very peeved about the 2001 Peace Accord between the NSCN (IM) and the Government of India. It stipulates a cease fire between the two on non-territorial premises. As an aftermath of this agreement in June 2001, the Meiteis ransacked the offices of the political parties in Imphal and even burnt down the historic Manipur Legislative building. The All Manipur Students Union (AMSU) also asked the members of the Legislative Assembly to resign from their seats (P.T.H. Jusho: 2004:28) Seeking guarantees from the Government of India that Manipur's territorial integrity would not be sacrificed on the altar of Naga peace has now become a major theme in Manipuri politics (Baruah: 2003: 321-338).

Oinam (*ibid.*) further states that in Manipur the ethnic conflicts can be seen between the earlier settlers and the later migrants. A distinct shift is now being witnessed in the State from the Meitei-centred confederation to tribe-centric movement.

Kshetri (2006: 151) writes that the Kukis did not fight only with the Nagas but also with the Paites who were demanding a separate identity. In June 1997, the Paites and the Kukis lost 214 lives due to skirmishes. Five thousand houses too were destroyed in the melee.

It is not that the militants were only able to target the security personnel, at times they too were targeted. At a seminar on November 10, 2006, in Delhi, Baboo Loifonbam, a human rights activist stated that during the year 2005, 64 extremists and 1,019 armed cadres were arrested in Manipur. During the same year police and security personnel had recovered 179 arms (with 5,500 ammunition), 48 hand grenades, 76 bombs, 249 detonators, 2,475 kg explosives and Rs. 17,00,000 cash. Thakura (2008) argues that violence in Manipur is due to political, economic and social factors. The political violence started when the merger agreement was signed with the Maharaja in 1949 under duress.

Whatever violence is being perpetrated by the militant groups in Manipur, it is nothing compared to the State repression. Hanjabam (2007) writes that there were 44,320 armed personnel of the central security forces stationed in the State. Taking into account of the total population of the State, there is one armed personnel for every 60 citizens. The figure does not include the State forces.

Tripura

In Tripura the main factor for ethnic upsurge is due to the massive influx of Bengali refugees from Bangladesh. The indigenous tribals have been reduced to just around 28 per cent in 1991 while they were around 58 per cent in 1951. Their lands have been alienated to the refugees. By the late 1960s, indigenous tribals had lost more than 60 per cent of their lands to immigrants (Fernandes: 2004). Frustrations due to land alienation and lack of employment opportunities have been the main factors of ethnic upsurge in the State.

The genesis of violence in Tripura can be traced back to the formation of Tripura Upajati Juba Samiti (TUJS) in June 1967. The main demands of it were:

1. Formation of autonomous district council for tribals;
2. Extension of inner-line regulation to Tripura;
3. Introduction of 'Kokborok' in Roman script as medium of instruction for tribal students; and
4. Restoration of alienated tribal lands.

The violent movements in Tripura later surfaced from 1970s. Tripura Upajati Juba Samiti or (TUJS) and Tripura National Volunteers (TNV) demanded an autonomous district council under Sixth Schedule in 1970s. This added fuel to the ongoing ethnic divide. In 1978, the tribal groups clashed with the Bengali ethnic institutions like Amra Bangali (Rajagopalan: 2008). The violence generated in the State is of protracted nature and it has caused untold sufferings to the people of all communities. The underground has made base on foreign soil and is supported by the tribesmen (S.R. Bhattacharjee: 1989).

The terror tactics was followed up by the TNV till 1988. An accord was signed with the government and underground led by Bijoy-Hrankhawal, a militant tribal leader. The agreement ensured that tribal lands will not be alienated any further. One-third of the seats in the State Legislature were to be reserved for tribals. This saw a period of relative lull in militancy. But some TNV members were not happy with the accord. The dissidents formed the All-Tripura Tribal Force in 1990. This group experienced a further split and violence escalated all-over the State. The violence continued in spite of a new agreement between the State Government and a faction of the All Tripura Action Force. The militant groups operate from the camps across the border in Bangladesh.

Bhaumik (2000: 149) states that in Tripura more than 1,20,000 Bengalese have been displaced due to guerrilla attacks and frequent massacres since 1980. In 1980, at Mandai, 324 people were killed. More than 4,000 people—mostly Bengalese, have been killed or kidnapped for ransom by tribal guerrilla groups like the National Liberation Front of Tripura (NLFT) or the All Tripura Tiger Force (ATTF)—in seven years time. Both the groups were opposed to the Bengalese as it led to physical, cultural, political and economic marginalization of the indigenous tribesmen. The ATTF has drawn the support of some pro-left youth but others are opposed to communism. In certain areas the Bengalese have retaliated and set fire to tribal villages or lynched the tribals. A Bengali militant organization called United Bengali Liberation Force (UBLF) too was formed. They even attacked the tribal people in buses or even on streets and terrorized them to leave the area predominated by the Bengalese, even in the suburbs of Agartala, the State capital.

H.N. Das (2007) endorses the fact that the Tripura Upajati Sena rocked Tripura for a long time resulting in the death of large number of Bengali people and damages of property belonging to individuals and institutions.

On 15th August, 2003 (Home World: August 16, 2003) 30 people, mostly Bengali settlers were killed in separate incidents. The worst militant violence took place in Totabari, a village in west Tripura district. There the rebels belonging to the All Tripura Tiger Force (ATTF) killed seven people on the spot around 9.30 P.M. Seven other people hit by arms succumbed on the way to the hospital.

In Tripura, the militants have adopted kidnapping for seeking ransom as one of the most important strategies to sustain themselves. Almost 70 per cent of the kidnapping cases in North-East are reported from Tripura (Kumar: 30). Bhaumik (2000) writes that the Tripura National Volunteers (TNV) and the Sengkrak continue with their tirade with the Bengali refugees. Between 1995 and 2003, 2,000 abduction cases were reported to the police. Many of those kidnapped failed to return even after the families paid a ransom. The government was compelled to change the succession laws, since the head could not be declared dead until the body was found, the banks and financial institutions would not accept the legal authority of the successors. With the change of laws, a person missing for a particular period of time is treated as dead in the eyes of the law to allow for succession. Many criminal gangs have got involved into the racket and selling off victims to militant outfits for higher ransom.

The political wing of the ATTF, Tripura People's Democratic Front (TPDF) has set up a parallel government in some remote areas of the State. As per reports, Tripura has become a corridor for pushing arms into other States in the North-East. The arms come from South-East Asian countries like Thailand and Singapore. The militant outfits too are involved in the supply of arms.

Quite like the other North-East States, factions within the militant parties are very much visible. The National Liberation Front of Tripura (NLFT) has been divided on religious lines. The Christians have resented the overbearing attitude of the Tripuris who attacked the Reangs. The Jamatiya tribes have now created their own set-up.

The Indigenous People's Front of Tripura (IPFT), formerly the political unit of NLFT approached the central Government for political settlements. Following this, there were a number of surrenders of the militants. The State also stepped up the counter-insurgency operations and declared the State as a disturbed area. In January 2000, the Government decided to implement the provisions of National Security

Act (NSA) to curb the upsurge in the State. The state of violence in Tripura thus continues as yet but in a much subdued manner as State administration has taken control of things and development activities have gained a firm footing.

Mizoram

The Mizos are the most predominant tribe of Mizoram. Mizos are divided into a number of sub-tribes like Lusei, Ralte, Hmar. Though these groups are numerically predominant in their pockets of concentration, they are not the indigenous peoples of Mizoram. Majority of them had migrated into the area from the Chin Hills and Burma in course of the last two centuries. They had displaced the indigenous Reangs or Tuikuks. The British promoted the Sailo chiefs belonging to the Lusei tribe. This resulted into the formation of Sailo chiefship, particularly in central and northern parts of Mizoram. After independence, chiefship was abolished and Village Councils were formed for managing the village affairs. The forests and lands were also taken over by the State.

The abolition of chiefship created a vacuum and the village community granaries where food used to be stored for the distress periods like village fire, natural calamities, famine, etc., were no longer maintained by the Village Council. As a consequence during the 1959 '*Mautam*'—blooming of the bamboo flowers and rapid procreation of hundred thousand rats that invaded the agricultural fields and devoured off the standing crops over night like locusts, a famine situation had arisen. The communication system was extremely poor in the Mizo Hills at that time and no relief material could reach most areas of the State. This created a lot of frustration and the Mizos formed a party called Mizo National Famine Front (MNFF) in September 1960, under the leadership of Laldenga. Within a short span of time, the MNFF changed into a political party called Mizo National Front. The MNF in turn formed an armed group called Mizo National Army on October 22, 1961. The MNA gathered weapons from abroad and made base camps in the forests and also in Myanmar and Bangladesh. The underground army collected tax from the outsiders staying in the State (Goswami: 1979). The government servants were charged 5 per cent of their salaries and the businessmen had to pay 10 per cent of their profit. It also raised local donations. In 1966, the MNA made a major attack on the security forces.

Nag (2008) states that the main target of MNF was the Assam Rifles concentration in Aizawl and the treasury offices of the government. On 28th February, 1960 till March 1966 about 800-1300 armed MNA cadres took part in the violence. In 1966, the MNA attacked Aizawl, Lunglei, Vairengte, Chaungte, Chimluang, Kolasib, Champai, Saireng and Demagiri simultaneously. The MNA looted treasury, kidnapped government officials, killed security personnel, damaged property and set fire to the bazaar. They disrupted communication and blocked roadways to prevent the Indian army from reaching the Mizo Hills. Within hours of the attack on March 1, 1966, the MNF declared independence and formed a government with Laldenga as the President of Mizoram.

The Indian security forces retaliated heavily and regrouped more than 400 villages. The villages from the remote forest areas were uprooted and brought and settled along with roadside villages. In the process houses in the native villages along with the churches were defiled and burnt down. 80 per cent of the people were thus affected. In new roadside villages the Mizos were compelled to build bamboo stockades all-around the peripheries of the settlements. People were provided with passes to go out and get into the villages when visiting agricultural fields. The villagers were also forced to do periodic *ntlang*—clearing off the thickets on the roadside so as to prevent the security forces being ambushed. Regrouping left deep psychological scars in the mentality of the people, and it is a trauma that many have not yet recovered from to this day (Internet). Many of the youths affected by regrouping joined the MNA. Roy (2008) writes that the counter-insurgency operations in Mizoram caused the extinction of one generation of young Mizos between 1966 and 1986.

Four types of regrouped villages were created by the security forces (B.B. Goswami: 1979)—(a) Progressive and Protected Village (PPV)—the first stage of grouping was done sometimes in the early part of 1967 in 19 centres; (b) New Grouping Centres (NGC)—These were accomplished in the later part of 1967 along the borders of Bangladesh; (c) Enlarged Loop Area (ELA)—initiated by the 59 Mountain Brigade operating from Manipur. These were started in 1967 and ended in 1968 along the Manipur-Burma border; and (d) Voluntary Group Centres (VGC)—initiated by 61 Mountain Brigade in scattered pockets except the entire southern pocket predominated by Pawi-Lakher tribes.

The security forces perpetrated tremendous oppression on the local people and ordinary citizens. A security camp was established on the top of every village to monitor the movements of the people. Houses were also raided at nights to search the militants. The government went to the extent of using the Air Force to bomb the suburbs of Aizawl on 5th and 6th March, 1966. But the Mizo National Army was not deterred from its activities and it led a successful guerilla warfare against the security forces from their jungle bases (Raghavaiah: 1977). They could create stirs even in urban centres. In one incidence of 1975 in Aizawl, the State capital, three of the top police officials of the region were mowed down by the militants in the Police Headquarters where they were in a meeting. The region witnessed a turbulence for almost twenty years until the Mizo Accord was signed between the MNF led by Laldenga and the Centre on June 30, 1986. Mizoram attained a full statehood in February 1987. But as yet the State continues to witness certain rumblings, particularly, in the border areas.

One very important lesson from the Mizoram experience is that should there be more unity among the militants, the chances of peace accords are higher.

Kshetri (2006: *op. cit.*) states Mizoram too has witnessed inter-ethnic fights. The dominant Mizos have attacked the Reangs dwelling in the southern part of Mizoram for quite a long time. The Reangs had to flee to the adjoining State of Tripura on several occasions. In the 1990s, hundreds died in makeshift camps where medicine, food and even shelter were scarce. But a Reang rebel group called the Bru National Liberation Front started demanding the formation of an autonomous council for the Reangs. During the height of the underground movement, the Indian Government had propped up the Shanti Bahini—an armed outfit of the Chakmas in the Chittagong Hill Tracts in Bangladesh to target the MNF bases (Bhaumik: *op. cit.*: p. 32).

A serious discord is to be observed in the North and North-East parts of Mizoram, the Hmars, a powerful tribe, has been demanding a separate State by incorporating the Hmar predominated contiguous areas of Mizoram, Manipur and Assam. Initially, they demanded the incorporation of the Hmar language. Later, they demanded full statehood. The Hmars have accumulated considerable arms and weapons and are regularly involved in armed onslaughts.

The Hmars were unhappy at the very beginning of the Mizo Accord in 1986 as the demand for Greater Mizoram was not acceded and adjoining Hmar areas were not consolidated. Consequently, the Hmar People's Convention was formed (HPC which came into existence in 1986) got split and HPC-D came into being. In 1992, HPC representatives and Government of Mizoram had signed a Memorandum of Settlement (MOS) on July 27, 1994 so as to form the 'Singlung Development Council'. 308 Hmar militants surrendered their weapons on the occasion.

The HPC-D, is, however, still sustaining. They get substantial financial support through extortions from the timber merchants. They also get international support for protecting the cause of the Christian Hmars. The outfit had in the initial stages drawn linkage with the NSCN and received weapons and training from it. Later on, it established linkages with the PLA in Manipur, as well. In May 2001, HPC-D joined the People's Revolutionary Alliance (IPRA)—a platform of the five Zo ethnic militant groups: the Zomi Reunification Organization (ZRO), two factions of the Kuki National Front, the KNF-P and KNF-MC, the Kuki National Army (KNA). However, there was a clash between HPC-D and ZRA—the armed wing of ZRO, and a truce was signed later in 2004.

The Nagas

Among the Nagas violence had been endemic. Biswas and Suklabaidya (*op. cit.*: 2008: p. 43) write that the Angami Naga believed in the past that the head-hunting and the subsequent sharing of flesh leads to a good harvest—this is a mode of symbolic return. The metaphoric play of the word 'return' not only signifies return in terms of a rich harvest, but also a return to the victorious, in the spirit of being useful to them. In other words, in terms of the Angami belief, the appropriation of the 'head' in the course of head-hunting was beginning of a new cycle of creation.

According to Shimray (2005), the Naga Movement cannot be considered to be a insurgent movement as the Nagas are not fighting for their independence but for recognition of being an independent country. The Naga movement precedes the independence of India. The Nagas had submitted a memorandum to the Simon Commission in 1929 that they should be left alone should British leave India.

But as things did not change, the Nagas have been fighting the Indian security forces for over fifty years now. The Nagas were apprehensive about the association of Naga predominated areas with

India for quite a long time—even before independence. The Nagas expressed their fear in 1947 that their culture—their ancient laws and customs and village organizations which they had retained would be destroyed by the Hindu rulers of India. They argued that a Constitution drawn by the people who have no knowledge of Nagaland and Naga people will be quite unsuitable and unacceptable to the Naga people. Thrown upon 100 crores of Indians, the one million Naga with their unique system of life, will be wiped out of existence. They, therefore, demand a separate independent State outside Indian Union. U. Misra (2006) echoes in the same vein: "The Naga leadership maintained that since the Nagas had never been part of India, the question of their secession from the country did not arise. Theirs was a national struggle for independence, and not a secessionist movement".

In 1950, the NNC rejected the Indian Constitution adopted in 1950 and held a plebiscite in May 1951 to decide whether the Nagas wanted to live in India or to secede (Become independent). The vote was 99.9 per cent in favour of independence. In response to a call from NNC, there was a total boycott of the general election in 1952 by the Nagas. Not a single nomination was filed, not to speak of votes. The 1957 general election too was boycotted.

According to Bhaumik (2007) Nehru ordered a repressive action after the Nagas boycotted the 1952 General Elections. P. Biswas and C. Suklabaidya (2008: 172) state that massive counter-insurgency operations were undertaken by the Indian State since 1954 and this led to widespread killing and bloodshed. N.K. Das (1982) too corroborates this. One of the worst incidents took place at Yangpang, Chingmei and Chemong villages. In Yangpang alone 60 men, women and children were butchered by the Indian Army. Naga Nationalist Council (NNC) held the army responsible for massacres, burning of villages, rape and all forms of destruction. The militants also retaliated and captured several weapons and even shot down an Indian Air Force plane. The authors further state that quite often the innocent people became victims of violent operations of both the State security forces as well as the militants. U.A. Shimray (2007) too has corroborated this.

In 1955, Assam Disturbed Areas Act was introduced to further strengthen the military offensive. The Naga problem was handled until the 1970s by the Ministry of External Affairs and not by the Home Ministry. Even in the eyes of the Indian Government, the Nagas constituted an external foe to be conquered rather than Indian citizens to be subdued (Nationalities on War-Path: A Selection of Vanguard Essays: Vanguard Publications: 1996: Kohima).

The late Prime Minister, Jawaharlal Nehru admitted on the floor of the Lok Sabha that the Nagas suffered 1,568 casualties between December 1958 and July 1959—in a period of just eight months.

On March 22, 1956, the Naga Nationalist Council (NNC) inaugurated its government—the Federal Government of Nagaland. Within two months it had raised a standing Army called the Naga Safe Guards. This army attacked the Indian army outposts at several places on March 24, 1956. The underground government in 1957 tried to negotiate with the Government of India. In the same year a Naga Peace Convention (NPC) was formed and through its negotiations an independent State of Nagaland was formed. But this did not satiate the aspiration of the Nagas and the violence continued to exist. The formation of Nagaland in 1963 did not permit consolidation of all Naga inhabited areas in Assam, Arunachal Pradesh and Manipur. In 1964, a Naga Peace Mission was formed (Through the efforts of the Baptist church) under the leadership of Jayprakash Narayan. But the Peace Mission tumbled due to the violation of cease fire as was agreed upon. Jayprakash Narayan resigned from the Mission as he felt that the FGN had no faith in him. Shimray (2005) brings into notice that the pro-Shillong Accord group formed its own militia—People's Militia of Nagaland (PMN) in tacit understanding with the Government of India. This outfit spread a reign of terror for quite some time in the Ukhrul area of Manipur and levied heavy taxes from the areas harbouring pro-NSCN stand.

Within a short time, rifts emerged within the Naga Federal Government itself mainly due to the differences between the Angami and Sema tribes. The Semas formed their own organization called 'Council of Naga People' and formed the 'Revolutionary Government of Nagaland' in 1968.

After the formation of Bangladesh in 1971, the Naga Movement received a severe jolt. In 1973, the security forces made a severe attack on the Naga underground—Naga Federal Army. Subsequently in 1975, the Shillong Accord was signed. However, the Accord was considered to be a sell out to the Government of India and a new party called National Socialist Council of Nagaland (NSCN) was formed. NSCN perpetrated tremendous violence against the security forces and civilians as well. But the party itself suffered from a rift and two parties were formed. One led by Khaplang (A Konyak Naga born in Myanmar) came to be known as NSCN(K) and the other led by Issac Swu (A Sema Naga) and T. Muivah (A Tangkhul from Manipur) became popularly known as NSCN(IM). Both the parties have been bitterly fighting with each other and several lives have been lost. The government at times has taken advantage of this. A. Shimray (2005) too supports this contention and writes that with the support of Government of India a youth outfit called Nagaland Youth Liberation Front (NYLF) was formed in 1990 to counter the NSCN. The Khaplang faction of NSCN served 'quit notice' to Tangkhuls staying in Mokokchung district. Quit notice was also served to Semas and Tikhirs in Kiphire area and lately Tangkhuls were asked to leave Kohima. Several Tangkhul lives were also taken.

The bitter war between the NSCN(IM) and NSCN(K) is quite well known (Rajagopalan: 2008). The Naga violence, however, escalated even after a Naga unification party was launched in 1997. Some of the breakaway cadres from NSCN(IM) are in the forefront of the organization. This group has been trying to bridge the differences between NSCN(IM) and NSCN(K). But at times met with violent attacks from the NSCN(IM). In August 2008 itself one of the NSCN(U) cadres was killed by the NSCN(IM) near Kuhuboto town in Dimapur district. In another incident in 2008, 11 Sumi tribesmen belonging to NSCN(U) were gunned down by the NSCN(IM) faction.

The NSCN(IM) has a formidable arsenal of weapons including AK-47, M-16, G-3-rifles, LMG, Russian built RPG-7 Rocket launchers, Grenade firing rifles, 2 inch mortars, hand grenades in addition to a large number of other assorted weapons and ammunition. The NSCN captured around 227 weapons from the Nagaland Armed Police in a year between 1993 and 1994. There are also reports that many Naga police have deserted their posts and joined the NSCN with weapons.

NSCN(IM) has adopted a strategy to tie up with other militant groups in the North-East. It decided to form a common front called 'Self Defence United Front of the South East Himalayan Region'. It has also tied up with foreign revolutionary groups like the Arakan Liberation Party (ALP), New Mon State Party (NMSP).

A. Shimray (2005: 255) states that the government enacted several draconian laws to contain the Naga Movement. Between 1953 and 1955 itself, the Assam Government enacted two special Acts—the Assam Maintenance of Public Order (Autonomous District) Act 1953 and the Assam Disturbed Area Act 1955. This was followed by the promulgation of the Armed Forces (Special Powers) Regulations 1958. The Armed Forces (Assam and Manipur) Special Powers Ordinance 1958 was later converted to an Act as the Armed Forces (Assam and Manipur) Special Powers Act 1958. This was later amended as the Armed Forces (Special Powers) Act 1972, to make it applicable to all the States and Union Territories in the North-East. Besides, other general laws like the National Security Act (NSA) and Terrorist and Disruptive (Prevention) Act (TADA) are too in operation. According to Human Rights activists, the main purpose of these Acts is to equip the security forces with excessive powers, putting themselves beyond the limits set by the Constitution of India.

Right from the 1950s, the security forces have brutally attacked the Naga army as well as the ordinary civilians. Thousands of lives have been lost and property destroyed. According to Biswas (2007), the Oinam case is one of the most notorious one of comparatively the more recent times. Army had launched the "Operation Blue Bird' in and around 21 villages including Oinam, in Manipur. (Insurgency, State Response and Society in North-East India). The case was brought to

Table 3.1: Security Situations in Nagaland

	1997	*1998*	*1999*	*2000*	*2001*
Incidents	380	202	294	195	128
Extremists killed	206	69	118	84	65
Extremists Arrested	129	64	39	81	80
Security Personnel killed	38	14	4	4	1
Arms looted	37	13	15	—	—
Arms recovered	50	18	16	86	96
Extremists surrendered	15	36	6	25	59
Civilians killed	97	26	26	13	16

Table 3.2: Security Situations in Manipur

	1997	*1998*	*1999*	*2000*	*2001*
Incidents	425	255	281	245	265
Extremists killed	151	95	78	102	170
Extremists Arrested	435	267	142	117	577
Security Personnel killed	111	62	64	51	26
Arms looted	74	58	147	140	16
Arms recovered	211	95	65	78	74
Extremists surrendered	13	1	1	33	7
Civilians killed	233	87	89	93	65

Table 3.3: Security Situations in Tripura

	1997	*1998*	*1999*	*2000*	*2001*
Incidents	303	586	616	826	370
Extremists killed	17	26	22	38	30
Extremists Arrested	154	399	335	798	547
Security Personnel killed	50	25	42	17	36
Arms looted	47	6	26	14	23
Arms recovered	95	154	76	137	95
Extremists surrendered	437	3	57	95	373
Civilians killed	220	229	248	360	237

Ref.: *Political Violence and the Police in India* by K.S. Subramanian, Sage, 2007.

the notice of the United Nations. Government of India was forced to constitute the National Human Rights Commission after this in 1994.

The Nagas did not lie low for long after the introduction of the Indian Army in 1950s. Phizo, the supreme Naga leader fled to London *via* East Pakistan (Now Bangladesh) to internationalize the issue of Naga people. The Naga National Council (NNC) created an armed wing, the Naga Army, and a parallel government—Federal Government of Nagaland (FGN). Many Naga youths were given training in East Pakistan and given weapons. By 1962, the Naga Army had 5,000 trained guerrillas backed by a less equipped support force of about 15,000 militia men.

Bhaumik (p. 10). The Naga insurgency can be classified into *four* broad phases:

1. 1957-64, phase when Pakistan trained rebels intensified the guerrilla war in Naga Hills.
2. The 1964-75 phase, when the movement peaked and weakened after two splits along tribal lines, ending with the signing of the Shillong Accord in 1975.
3. 1975-1987 phase—during which NNC split and NSCN emerged.
4. Post-1987 phase when NSCN also split along tribal lines and both faction tried negotiating with the government.

NSCN (IM), the most powerful Naga underground militant group has made some very successful assaults on the Indian security forces through guerrilla tactics. It has killed scores of soldiers and seized large cache of arms. Since 1992-93 almost all the areas inhabited by the Nagas, including Tirap and Changlang districts of Arunachal Pradesh come under the effective control of NSCN(IM). It also received international recognition and has become a member of the Unrepresented Nations of People's Organisation (UNPO) in January 1953 (Vanguard Publications: 1996). The Government of Peoples' Republic of Nagaland has also established links with the UN Working Group on Indigenous People (UNWGIP) (Tables 3.1 to 3.3).

Lasuh (2002: 176-184) narrates an incidence of the States' attitude towards the local Nagas *vis-à-vis* the security forces. In 1952, a Naga leader was killed by an Indian officer in Kohima. Nagas demanded an inquiry Commission. Accordingly, a Commission was constituted but it sent twelve Nagas to jail and a concerned Indian officer was reported to have been promoted. Lasuh further states that physical beating was not enough and the Indian Government took resort to using the services of the Indian Air Force. Villages were razed down, houses and schools were pulled down and people tortured to death. Mangmetong village with 365 houses was attacked twenty one times. Khensa village with 314 houses was attacked 19 times in one year. Property was looted. Granaries were destroyed and people restrained to the fields for cultivation. Between January 1955 to July 1957, 79,794 houses were burnt down, 2,65,50,000 maunds of paddy-rice destroyed, rupees 96,00,00,000 things were lost due to fire in 612 villages out of 852 Naga villages. Lasuh, also writes, that Naga women have been subjected to torture and rape, e.g., a mad woman named Khololi of Ratomi village aged 40 years was raped on November 9, 1956, led by Commandant Mickey of the Garhwal Regiment. The army even sodomized the young Naga boys.

The limit of the heinous crimes perpetrated by the Indian security personnel knows no bound. They went to the extent of frying alive the Naga people in military outposts in Nagaland. For instance, one Mr. Khehoto, aged 52, was fried to death at Maru outpost in March 1957. There are also reports that Naga victims were captured and put on the nettle leaves, and watered throughout the day and night till the life expired.

The violence in Naga dominated areas have not been only due to confrontation with the State security forces but also due to the fact there have been virtual fratricide between the different tribes. After the 1988 split in NSCN, due to fratricidal wars more than 200 NSCN(IM) and NSCN(K) fighters were killed. After serious set backs in 1994-95, the NSCN(IM) decided to have negotiations with the

Government of India since 1997. The Indian Security Forces did not intervene even when both the groups were using heavy weapons like mortar. In many places in Nagaland like Phek, people becoming fed up with factional feuds, chased away both the groups of NSCN. Though criticizing each other both the factions have built contacts with the security forces and intelligence wing.

M.Z. Rahman (2008) writes that the Sema Nagas suffered immensely due to the differences with the Tangkhul dominated NSCN(IM) and they joined the Khaplang faction of NSCN. Encounters between the two led to seventy deaths in the past three months...." NSCN(IM) has used cease fire to their own benefit by attacking NSCN(U), and blamed them for the violence. Carrying arms under the jackets and shawls everywhere during cease fire, which has been done by NSCN(IM) defeats the very rationale of having a cease fire, as it can lead to violence anytime.

According to B.B. Kumar, the Naga militants have splintered into several factions and people's loyalties have become divided between NSCN(IM), NSCN(K) and NNC. Their outlook towards the nation is not similar. Each Naga tribe has its own tradition and identity. These would not, therefore, permit all the Naga nationalities to have one identity and work under the umbrella of one organization, say the NSCN(IM).

S.K. Roy (2008) writes that in the present days the general public is getting wary of the militants and are even retaliating back. "People do react back spontaneously when their patience is stressed too far. In the second week of September 2003, the common people of Mokokchung in Nagaland assaulted the NSCN(K) cadres and refused to pay 'tax' to them. The public burst out in anger when NSCN cadres shot at a student and two others. The homes and vehicles of top leaders were torched and the group ordered its men to hold their fire, worried that the situation would worsen. The local leader left away to another township along with his family members and party colleagues.

Conclusion

It is apparent from the above review of literature that the violence in North-East India in the post-Independence period is a genesis of the past. It is rooted to colonial conquest of the British and travesty of formation of the Indian nation-state. Though the region has a large section of people belonging to the Mongoloid stock, the widespread violence is not due to any racial discrimination. For instance, the ULFA draws its support mainly from the ethnic Assamese. Neither does the violence depict any class war. The violence is at best indicative of a great deal of anti-State stance and inter-ethnic conflagrations—to a great deal due to waves of migrations. This is most clearly evident in the case of Naga movement where the Nagas are waging a freedom movement on the one hand and on the other are involved in internecine infantile war. The Bodos are similarly pitted against the state as well as the divided ethnic entities.

It would be infantile to blame the local people of the North-East for the vitriolic bouts of violence. It is rather the State which is largely responsible for the perpetual strife. Way back in 1929, when the Naga Club was formed, the Nagas had indicated their worry of becoming marginalized if merged with India (That has a very large population). Precisely so, due to the population logic rationalizing the formation of electoral constituencies, the North-East region has just 25 seats in the Lok Sabha, while Uttar Pradesh alone has 80 seats. More than anything, the Government of India has turned the entire North-East into a virtually military State. Other than the draconian Acts and enactments, the military presence is of alarming proportion. It is a pity that the people of other parts of the country fail to register the feelings of the people that region several battalions of security personnel (Most of whom belong to North India) were pushed into Assam following the killing of Hindi-speaking labourers.

Whatever may be the fallout of the North-East militancy, it has triggered a chain action and a large number of armed upsurges have come up not only among the hill peoples but also among many tribal and non-tribal peoples in the plains. A positive outcome of the militancy is that traditional land rights, particularly in the hills, have not been much disrupted and alienated as in many other parts of India. It has also generated consciousness among the new generations to fathom the meaning of nation-state—it is not to be viewed as a hegemonic order of the ethnic majority. However, the local people are always apprehensive of the government designs. Already thousand of outside labourers have entered into Arunachal Pradesh for the Subansiri river dam project. Disaster is awaiting them as several other hydropower projects will be coming up in course of the next decade. A few sections of the youth in the State have already turned restive.

REFERENCES

A Syndicated Report, (1995), *North-East India and the Indian State: Paradoxes of a Periphery*, New Delhi: Vikas.

Baruah, S. (1986), "Immigration, Ethnic Conflict and Political Turmoil in Assam 1979-1985", *Asian Survey*, Vol. 26, No. 11, November.

Baruah, S. (2002), "Gullivers's Troubles: State and Militants in North-East India" in *EPW*, October 12.

Baruah, S. (2003), "Citizens and Denizens: Ethnicity, Homelands and The Crisis of Displacement in North East India" in *Journal of Refugee Studies*, Vol. 16, No. 1, 2003.

Baruah, S. (2003), "Confronting Constructionism Ending India's Naga War" in *Journal of Peace Research*, Vol. 40, No. 3, May.

Baruah, S. (2007), *Post Frontier Blues: Towards a New Policy Framework for Northeast India*, Washington: East-West Centre.

Bates, R. *et al.* (2002), "Organizing Violence" in *The Journal of Conflict Resolution*, Vol. 46, No. 5, October.

Bhadra, R. (2007), "Ethnic Identity Problem and Administrative Efficacies in North-East India" in R.K. Bhadra and Mita Bhadra eds. *Ethnicity, Movement and Social Structure: Contested Cultural Identity*; Jaipur: Rawat.

Bhattacherjee, S.R. (1989), *Tribal Insurgency in Tripura*, New Delhi: Inter-India.

Bhaumik, S. (2000), "Negotiating Access: Northeast India" in *Refugee Survey Quarterly*; Vol. 19. No. 2.

Bhaumik, S. (2007), *Insurgencies in India's Northeast: Conflict, Cooperation and Change*, Washington: East-West Working Paper, July 10.

Biswas, S. (2007), "Insurgency, State Response and Society in North-East India" in R.K. Bhadra and Mita Bhadra eds. *Ethnicity, Movement and Social Structure: Contested Cultural Identity*; Jaipur: Rawat.

Biswas, P. and Suklabaidya, C. (2008), *Ethnic-Worlds in North-East India: An Analysis*, New Delhi: Sage.

Budha, K. (2008), "Terrorism, Bandrillard and a Death in North East India", Subaltern Studies *http://subalternstudies-con/?p=401*).

Damzen, J. (2008). "Response of the Youth to the Karbi-Kuki Conflict in Karbi-Anglong" in L. Jeyseelam ed. *Conflict Mapping and Peace Process in North-East India*; Guwahati: North Eastern Social Research Centre.

Das, H.N. (2007). "Ethnic Aspirations and Insurgency in North-Eastern Region of India" in B.B. Kumar ed. *Problems of Ethnicity in the North-East India*; New Delhi: Concept.

Das, N.K. (1982), "The Naga Movement" in K.S. Singh ed. *Tribal Movements in India*; New Delhi: Manohar.

Das, S.K. (2007), "Conflict and Peace in India's Northeast: The Role of Civil Society", Occasional Paper; Washington D.C.: East-West.

Dasgupta, A. (2001), "Small Arms Proliferation in India's North-East: A Case Study of Asia", *EPW*, January 6.

Dasgupta, J. (1997), "Community, Authenticity and Autonomy and Institutional Development in India's North-east" in *The Journal of Asian Studies*, Vol. 52, No. 2 May.

Fernandes, W. (2004), "Limits of Law and Order Approach to the North-East", *EPW*, October 16.

George, S.J. (1994), "The Bodo Movement in Assam: Unrest to Accord, *Asian Survey*, Vol. 34, No. 10 (October).

Goswami, B.B. (1979), *The Mizo Unrest*, Jaipur: Aalekh Publishers.

Hanjabam, S.S. (2007), "The Meitei Upsurge in Manipur" in *AEJ*, DOI 10.

Haokip, D.M. (2008), "Kuki-Naga Conflict in Special Reference to the Chandel District of Manipur" in L. Jeyseelam ed. *Conflict Mapping and Peace Process in North-East India*; Guwahati: North Eastern Social Research Centre.

Henderson, E.A. (1999), "Ethnic Conflict and Cooperation", *Encyclopedia of Violence, Peace and Conflict*, Vol. 1, San Diego: Academic Press.

Iralu, K.D. (2003), *Nagaland and India: The Blood and the Thorns*, Kohima: K.D. Iralu.

Jusho, P.T.H., (2004), *Politics of Ethnicity in North East India, with Special Reference to Manipur*, New Delhi: Regency Publications.

Kindo, C. and Minj, D. (2008), "Impact of Assam-Nagaland Territorial Dispute in District of Golaghat, Assam" in L. Jeyaseelam ed. *Conflict Mapping and Peace Process in North-East India*; Guwahati: North Eastern Social Research Centre.

Kshetri, R. (2006), *The Emergence of Meitei Nationalism*, New Delhi: Mittal Publications.

Kumar, B.B. (2007), "Ethnicity and Insurgency in North-East India" in B.B. Kumar ed. *Problems of Ethnicity in North-East India*; New Delhi: Concept.

Lasuh, W. (2002), *The Naga Chronicle*, New Delhi: Regency Publications.

Leach, C.W. (1999) "Ethnicity and Identity Politics" in *Encyclopaedia of Violence, Peace and Conflict*, Vol. 1, San Diego: and Academic Press.

Brown, L.M.; Misra, U., (2000), *The Periphery Strikes Back*, Shimla: IIAS.

Misra, U. (2006), "The Margin Strikes Back: Echoes of Sovereignty and the Indian State" in G. Sen (ed.) *Where the Sun Rises When Shadows Fall: The North-East*, New Delhi: OUP.

Nag, S. 1996 (2008), *Pied Pipers in North-East India: Bamboo Flowers Rat Famine and the Politics of Philanthropy*—1881-2007; New Delhi: Manohar.

Nangengast, (1994), "Violence, Terror and the Crisis of the State" in Annual Review. *Anthropol.* 23: 109-36.

Nardi, D.J. (2008), "Cross-Border Chaos: A Critique of India's Attempts to

Index